PENGUIN HANDBOOK
THE PLAYGROUP BOOK

Marie Winn is the author of several books for
children, the compiler and editor of the *FIRE-
SIDE BOOK OF CHILDREN'S SONGS,* and a
former playgroup mother. She was born in Prague
and is now an American citizen. She is married
to Allan Miller, conductor of Youth Programs of
Baltimore Symphony Orchestra, and they have
two children, aged six and three. Mary Ann
Porcher was born in Budapest and is now an
American citizen. She was educated at the University of Texas at El Paso, New York University,
and Bank Street College of Education, and as a
teacher, is a pioneer in the field of early childhood
education. She is married to Walter Porcher, a
newspaperman in New York, and they have a son,
aged ten.

The Playgroup Book

by

Marie Winn and
Mary Ann Porcher

Illustrations by STEPHEN SZOKE

PENGUIN BOOKS INC.
BALTIMORE, MARYLAND

Penguin Books, Inc
7110 Ambassador Road, Baltimore, Maryland
21207

First published by The Macmillan Co., New
York, 1967
Published by Penguin Books 1969

Printed by Kingsport Press, Inc., Kingsport,
Tennessee in the United States of America

Acknowledgment

MANY playgroup mothers played an important part in the writing of this book by reporting on their experiences and trying out on their groups many of the ideas found here. Special thanks are due to Billie Dolin, Marie Miller, Shirley Romaine and Mary Ellen Wang for taking part in the model playgroup used for The Playgroup Book, and for supplying four joyful playgroupers—Julie, Mikey, Jenny and Michael.

Grateful acknowledgment is also due to Mrs. Mildred Rabinow of the Child Study Association of America for her encouraging comments and most valuable suggestions; to Mrs. Anita Bookey for expert advice on various aspects of how young children learn; and to Mrs. Janet Malcolm for many practical ideas on group activities taken from her experiences with Kibbutz preschoolers.

Contents

PART II: *Activities*

Introduction

The purpose of this book

THE PLAYGROUP BOOK was written to encourage and help mothers
run successful playgroups for their preschool children. These
mothers are not new to the ways of children. Indeed, they have
all had at least three years of experience in managing, protecting,
educating and enjoying one or more of their own. But they are
new to the ways of children in groups. This is a sphere usually
reserved for professionals: teachers, counselors and group leaders.
Yet an untrained mother *can* organize a most successful playgroup, enjoyable and valuable for the children involved and
rewarding for herself, as well. She needs to have some information about the nature of preschool children, however, in order
to know how best to manage such a group—she must know something about the activities young children like, and the best way
to supervise these activities.

This book is concerned with three- and four-year-olds, how
they are likely to behave in a group and how best to help them
adjust to a group experience. It shows how to help them achieve
the many advantages to be gained from playgroup membership.
It includes a variety of easy activities a mother can introduce to a
group of children. Wherever necessary, directions on the presenta-
tion of an activity to the playgroup for the first time are given,
often including the actual words a mother might use to explain it.

All the suggestions in this book are made in the light of current
knowledge about preschool children, their needs, interests and
amazing potential for learning. Specific ways to utilize playgroup activities to develop children's readiness for their future

education are included throughout the book. Most important, all the activities included are fun for preschoolers. They have been tested in many nursery schools and in a pilot playgroup set up especially for the purposes of this book.

How this book is organized

Part One deals with the fundamentals of running a playgroup. It includes chapters on the nature of the preschool child, how to equip and organize a playroom, how to prepare a child for joining a playgroup, how to deal with separation problems that might arise, and the actual mechanics of making a playgroup morning run smoothly. Part Two presents specific activities suitable for playgroup children in art, music, science, literature, block play, trips, nature study, dramatic play, and water and sand play. The Table of Contents, subdivided for easy reference, provides a quick idea of what each chapter contains.

How to use this book

Every playgroup mother will run her morning in a different way. Some will concentrate on a great variety of art activities. Others will have a talent for encouraging dramatic play and make-believe. Some will find singing and music activities most rewarding, others will specialize in science activities. Still others will do a little bit of everything during the course of a playgroup year.

Use this book as you would a cookbook: browse through it and try the activities that appeal to you most, and those that you think you can do best. There is no need to do everything, nor even almost everything. You can use activities exactly as suggested in this book, or you can invent variations.

The authors have tried to indicate which activities are better for older playgroupers and which for younger ones, but children and groups vary, so use your common sense in deciding what to do with your playgroup. If an activity sounds too hard for your particular group, don't try it.

Some of the activities presented here may not appeal to you because your child has tried them on his own and shown no interest or delight in them. You must remember, however, that an activity your child has tried alone becomes something quite different when done with a group of children; it may be worth trying again.

As a final note, there is nothing to prevent any mother, or for that matter any father, grandmother or babysitter, from using the ideas and activities suggested in this book for just one or two young children. The recommended ways for introducing activities or using them to help children learn are in most cases equally applicable to a single child.

PART I

Fundamentals

CHAPTER 1

The Value of a Playgroup

What is a playgroup?

FOUR or five preschool children who meet regularly at each other's homes to play, with each mother supervising the whole group in turn, make up a playgroup. A playgroup is *not* a babysitting arrangement. It is a small organization that is planned and prepared, with equipment supplied for the children's play and activities introduced by the mothers in charge. Undoubtedly it is a real job for each mother to do, requiring a certain amount of time and energy. But it can be an enormously rewarding experience for all the children involved, and also, by the way, for the mothers.

What the playgroup offers the child

A CHANCE TO BE WITH OTHER CHILDREN

Children of this age no longer play happily in their rooms as they did when they were babies. They should not be expected to. They want to be with other children, and even when they do not actually play *together*, their play takes on a different meaning when they *are* together.

LEARNING HOW TO GET ALONG WITH OTHERS

Children learn the necessity of sharing when the playgroup meets at their own house—sharing their toys and, what is more difficult, sharing their own mother when another child demands her attention. They begin to gain control over their feelings and learn to conform to the easy standards set for the playgroup. Their most important lessons are from each other; when one child waits his turn patiently instead of having a temper tantrum, the others are likely to follow his example. They are much more likely to imitate another child's behavior than to do what a grownup tells them to do.

A FEELING OF BELONGING TO A GROUP

"My playgroup" and "my playgroup friends"—after a playgroup has been running for a few weeks, these words begin to appear in your child's conversations. He feels some pride in having a special group of his own, where he is important by himself, not just as a member of a family. After a time the group itself begins to influence the social behavior of each child in it. The children begin to modify their behavior not just for their own advantage, at least not directly, but for the advantage of the whole group. A child will put away the toys he has been playing with when he sees the other children doing their jobs and when he knows that they will have to wait for him before the snack is served. Previously, his mother's demands that he put away his toys only made him refuse stubbornly. But now he belongs to the group and the group is more important to him, at this particular moment, than the necessity of asserting his own personality.

Naturally, in the course of a playgroup morning the children play individually some of the time; indeed, most of the time, at the beginning. But sooner or later they come together as a group—in a make-believe game, or at snack time, storytime or music time. These group times become more enjoyable and occur more frequently as the months go by and the children begin to feel themselves really part of a group. They learn that they have more fun when the group works and plays together and they really try to get along—as much as they can.

A STEP TOWARDS INDEPENDENCE

Most children of this age are ready to begin the weaning process from mother and home that ends with full-time attendance in school. The playgroup's limited size and informal atmosphere can make your child's first regular separation easy to manage. In most cases the fun of playing with other children outweighs the possible discomfort of leaving his mother. The child who has difficulties leaving his mother and accepting a playgroup is perhaps the child who needs to join a playgroup most of all: his difficulties might be greater in the larger, more formal world of a school. If he works out his problem within the framework of a playgroup, he will be more likely to adjust to school.

GETTING TO KNOW THE OTHER PLAYGROUP MOTHERS

The other playgroup mothers become an important part of your child's life. Their friendly interest in him and his achievements, their acceptance of him the way he is (often easier for them than for you, precisely because they are *not* his mother), their protection and support when necessary, will give your child a good foundation for his future relations with grownups. Each mother will have different ways of talking, reacting and dealing with problems.

As your child begins to accept these differences, he learns that there are many good ways of doing things, not just the way things are done at home. In his dealings with the other playgroup mothers, he is learning how grownups behave and think and, by their example, how to behave and think himself. Most of all, he is learning that grownups other than his parents can be liked and trusted and enjoyed.

ENJOYING ART MATERIALS

The preschooler has many deep feelings which he cannot yet express in words. The availability at each playgroup home of a wide variety of art materials and the freedom to use them fully, without adult-imposed standards, gives him a chance to express his feelings in a most enjoyable way. This is not to say that the playgroup is a form of therapy for disturbed children. Playgroup mothers are by no means encouraged to become amateur psychologists. But giving a normal child access to art materials supplies a healthy outlet for feelings that might otherwise get bottled up. What's more, all children love art activities, and gain a sense of achievement from actually making pictures and things.

BECOMING LESS SELF-CENTERED

Within the family your child is loved and valued no matter what he can or cannot do. His share of affection and attention is, hopefully, very large indeed. But in a group of children his own age, he will soon find that his position is not automatically secure; attention and respect must be earned. His position in the group depends on his behavior to the other children, on his powers and skills, on what he has to offer. He becomes aware that other people's reactions to him are more objective than those he receives at home. As a result, he begins to replace some of the self-centered behavior that has served him well until now with the give and take necessary for group life.

DEVELOPING SELF-CONFIDENCE

Your child's position in relation to you and other grownups is fairly powerless and dependent. No matter how child-centered a family may be or how secure the child, he still feels that his parents are big and strong and all-knowing and he is none of these. Belonging to a group of children his own age is a wonderful antidote to feeling small and helpless. Discovering that he is like other children, concerned with the same things, that he can do many things as well as they and perhaps some things better, helps your child develop the self-confidence that he needs in order to explore the possibilities of his world.

INTELLECTUAL DEVELOPMENT

With the help of well-selected equipment and the guidance of the mother in charge, your child will move along quickly in his efforts to understand the world outside himself. In many ways, he will be laying the foundations for academic subjects that will stand him in good stead when he begins school. Block play can introduce mathematics. A sign on a playhouse saying "Grocery Store" can be the first introduction to the idea that words are symbols for real things. Matching games that involve touching, listening or observing increase perception. A trip to the supermarket can be a basic lesson in economics. Three- and four-year-olds are perhaps at the very height of their eagerness to learn, and modern research is beginning to show that they are capable of learning and understanding a great deal more than was believed possible in the past. The playgroup can provide innumerable opportunities to extend your child's knowledge and understanding. The playgroup mother is always present to explain and interpret, correct misconceptions, provide more material when a child reveals a desire for learning more about something—most of all, to listen to the children and talk to them about their ideas.

The children themselves, however, without any grown-up help or participation, extend each other's horizons, exchange information and test each other's knowledge and understanding in conversations and in dramatic play.

FUN

This is first, last and foremost. Your child will have fun in a playgroup, much more fun than he would have alone at home. He will profit from it in many ways, but as far as he is concerned, he will be having a whale of a good time, and that is the best reason of all to send him to playgroup.

What the playgroup offers the mother

FREE TIME

The obvious advantage is three or four free mornings a week (free of *one* child, anyhow), in exchange for one morning when you are in charge of the playgroup. For mothers without much household help, this time off is most welcome.

INSIGHT

In observing the same group of children playing over a period of time, you will gain insight into the nature of the preschoolers usually reserved for nursery-school teachers and other professionals. You will get an idea of what behavior is typical for your child's age. You will have the fascinating experience of watching children learn and develop.

Moreover, you will get new perspective into *your* child's behavior and personality after seeing him playing with a group of his friends week after week. On the basis of your observations, you may find yourself adjusting your expectations for him. The reports from the other playgroup mothers about his behavior at their homes—the strong and weak points they may have observed—can add to your understanding of your child and reveal whole areas of interest that you never suspected.

CHAPTER 2

The Playgroup Child

AN IDEA of some typical characteristics of three- and four-year-olds, an understanding of what play means to them and the typical forms of their play, will be helpful in your dealings with a playgroup. It must be emphasized that the lists that follow apply to many children but by no means all, and the reasons for any disparity between your child and the list are many. A child who has had few opportunities to play with other children will probably not be as advanced in social skills as a child with many playmates already. Children with older brothers and sisters tend in some ways to be ahead of children who have none. And children vary enormously, just by nature. Some children may paint "real things" at two, while others are still painting abstractions at four. In neither case is there cause for rejoicing or alarm. The lists of typical characteristics are designed to give you an overall picture of the average three- and four-year-old, not to be specific guides to what children "ought" to be doing.

Characteristics of the playgroup child

THE THREE-YEAR-OLD

Better *physical control and coordination* than at two. No more toddling. Runs with long strides, jumps well, climbs steps one foot after another. Likely to fall on face when running. Cut lips very common.

Social interests growing. Wants to be with children his own age

or older, but will have nothing to do with babies. Hates to be
called "baby." Begins to form friendships, although these are
often fleeting. Does not usually care whether he plays with boys
or girls.

Social behavior improving. Is willing to share, sometimes. Finds
it difficult, but possible, to wait his turn. Reasonable about many
things, but cannot be depended upon to keep a "deal." Can be
terribly demanding, "bossy," and may still have an occasional
tantrum when interfered with, although not as often as at two.
Still needs a great deal of adult contact, may want to sit on a lap
when scared or insecure and wants to be comforted physically
when hurt. Can also be very detached at times and tries to
behave independently more and more.

Concentration usually better than at two. Still likes repetitive
activities such as stacking and sorting. Needs to have many
activities provided and will usually spend a short time at each.
Group activities must be short for this age.

Language is improving rapidly. Speaks in sentences. Talks a
lot to anyone who will listen and even to himself when no one
is around. Likes to learn new words and is interested in "big"
words. His pronunciation still has traces of "baby" in it, particularly *s* and *l* sounds; this may not vanish until four or five.
Likes to play with words and make rhymes. May begin to bring
home "bad words" and will repeat them if he gets a shocked
reaction.

Sense of time still vague. Can distinguish between night and
day, but may still confuse his nap with the night sleep and
yesterday with tomorrow. Understands the difference between
"soon" and "not for a long time." Beginning to get an idea about
seasons: summer is hot and winter is cold.

Bathroom habits are improving. May go to the bathroom by
himself if he can pull his pants down easily but usually asks
to go before he does. Many children still need to be reminded at
this age and will remain engrossed in play until it is too late.
The signs that a child needs to go to the bathroom are usually
very clear and a grownup can prevent most accidents by watch-

ing for them and reminding the child to go. Another frequent cause of wet pants at this age is laughing very hard.

FOUR-YEAR-OLD

Physical control quite good. Walks and runs more steadily than at three. Falls usually result in skinned knees and elbows. Increase in physical energy, much climbing, tussling and jumping.

Social behavior more sophisticated than at three. Much more give and take and cooperation possible. Special friendships begin to be formed, and even cliques. Boys begin to gravitate to boys and girls to girls for playing, except in make-believe games where there are male and female roles.

Discipline is more of a problem because the child is more aware of what he wants to do and thus harder to redirect to other activities. Often the only thing you can do is say "no," point blank. Tends to overdo everything physically: fills things to overflowing, performs dangerous feats to prove his prowess.

Language sophisticated and sometimes comically grown-up. Likes to make up silly words. Grammar and syntax quite mature.

Imagination is extremely vivid and often leads to fear and anxiety. Sees more possibilities of harm or danger and thus is more easily frightened than a three-year-old. May be very emotional.

Concentration is improving. Has a longer interest span than at three and may spend longer period of time at one activity. Interested in real stories and can sustain attention from beginning to end.

Dramatic play or make-believe takes up more of his play time. Needs more props for play than at three.

Accomplishments are many and he is proud of them: can dress himself almost entirely, except back buttons and shoelaces; can carry a tune quite well and knows many songs completely; is beginning to paint "real things" and the end result is more interesting to him than the actual process of painting. Can repeat some stories he has been told and is beginning to make up simple stories of his own. Can build elaborate block constructions and enjoys group building projects.

Sense of time developing. Has some conception of a minute, an hour, tomorrow, next week.

Bathroom habits usually good, but accidents are still far from uncommon and may be humiliating. This makes it even more important for a grownup to remind him to go to the bathroom if he is squirming or dancing. May absent-mindedly handle genitals when absorbed in some activity, especially when listening to stories or music.

About children's play

To most grownups the word "play" means a carefree and light-hearted amusement, an activity opposite to "work," the serious business of life. But to young children, play itself is the serious business of life. It is learning and practicing and testing —in short, it *is* work. Of course play is fun too, but it is not like adult recreation, since children spend virtually all their waking hours at it, in one form or another.

THE STAGES OF CHILDREN'S PLAY

Solitary play

Babies and very young children play by themselves much of the time, unconcerned with other children or grownups who may be around. They are interested in the materials they are playing with—how they feel, sound, taste and smell, and what they can do to and with these materials. They push and pull, take apart and try to put together, put things in and take them out, pile things up and knock them down. At some time around one they develop a primitive sense of play involving interaction: they drop objects and love to have them fetched by others or they will crawl after a ball someone throws to them.

Parallel play

Later, somewhere around two years, children begin to enjoy

playing near other children, although each of them will be involved in separate activities. Playing seems to be more fun when other children are around, even though they don't actually play together.

Social play

The next stage begins around the age of three, when children begin to play together in pairs or small groups. It is the need for this form of play that makes a playgroup important.

THE FORMS OF SOCIAL PLAY

Obviously there is a lot of overlapping in these stages of play. Older children still spend much time playing alongside each other, or even playing alone, oblivious to the world. But by the time your child is three, social play becomes increasingly important in his life and begins to take up a greater proportion of his playtime than the other forms of play. Social play usually falls into one of three categories: active or physical play, make-believe play and word play.

Active play

Much of the preschooler's play involves developing, practicing and perfecting physical skills. He climbs, jumps, runs, gallops, slides, rides, bounces, falls—for the sheer fun of doing it. But whereas this sort of practicing has been going on since infancy, the social aspect is now becoming important. "Let's jump and fall down, Jenny," says Peter, and they begin to jump and fall down over and over again, screaming with laughter at each fall. "Let's gallop like horses," and "Let's run to the corner and back," and "Let's do somersaults,"—activities which are no longer very interesting when done alone become fun with another child.

Make-believe play

Make-believe play is *the* great social activity of preschool children, the common ground where they can really play together. In their make-believe play children learn about the world, about themselves, about relationships. By re-enacting important experiences they try to understand them better. The little girl playing "mommy" in a game of house is not only preparing for motherhood twenty years hence, but she may be trying to understand why her own mommy was angry or upset that particular morning. When she gets angry at her "baby," she suddenly feels better about her own mommy's anger at her. Perhaps she understands the justice of it now. Or perhaps by getting angry herself, in play, she has evened the score. Best of all, you cannot play house alone; you need a mommy and a daddy and a baby too. Each child is needed to play a role, and the feeling of importance that comes from being needed is as satisfying to a child as it is to a grownup.

Word play

Conversation is an obvious social activity, and by three most children are beginning to talk together in simple ways. Much of the talk is exchange of information: "Guess what?" and "Do you know . . . ?" Three- and four-year-olds are also beginning to enjoy playing with the sounds and meanings of words. Children do this alone practically from the time they begin to talk, but now the social possibilities of word play become clear to them. For instance, while having juice and cookies Michael says, "I like chocolate cookies." To which Julie quickly replies "*I* like chocolate googies." All the children laugh and the game is started. "I like chocolate gagas," says Helen and everybody roars with laughter. "I like chocolate tricycles," says Julie, changing the nature of the game and a new height of merriment is reached. "I like chocolate overalls," and "I like chocolate googeralls," and so on. This activity often strikes grownups as foolish and incomprehensible, but it is a most valuable and satisfactory way of communicating for three-year-olds. The word games children invent are likely to become group jokes, repeated time and time again, and these become part of the common experience of the playgroup that helps them feel like a real group rather than four or five individuals thrown together.

CHAPTER 3

Organization

Getting your playgroup together

HOW MANY CHILDREN?

FOUR is perhaps the ideal number of children for a nursery playgroup. A playgroup of three children is possible, but group activities so important to the playgroup idea are hard to arrange for such a small number. Four children make a real group; they feel the difference between their playgroup playing and the casual playing they do when one or two children drop over. A playgroup of five children is fine, but many mothers feel unequal to the job of managing five children alone. Somehow, four seem less formidable. A confident, experienced mother can certainly manage five children as well as four, but a mother who is unsure of her abilities will probably feel happier limiting her playgroup to four.

WHAT AGES?

Most children are ready to join a playgroup when they are three. A few independent and verbal (and toilet-trained) two-and-a-half-year-olds are ready and will hold their own in a group of three-year-olds. It is best if the children are not more than six months apart in age, but many playgroups have worked well with mixed groups of threes and fours.

SEX DISTRIBUTION

Ordinarily the proportion of boys to girls is not important in a group of preschool children. If you end up with all children of one sex or two boys and two girls there are no problems. If, however, you end up with a single boy in a group of girls or vice versa, it is important to look at the single child's personality to see if he or she will fit in with the group. A tough, tomboyish girl will probably do perfectly well in a group with three boys, but a very feminine little girl might miss a companion to play at dolls with. Similarly, a very athletic, transportation-minded boy might feel out of place in a group of four feminine, motherly little girls.

Choosing the other mothers for your playgroup

The standards you use in choosing playgroup mothers need not be the same one you use in making friends; you don't have to look for philosophical, political or intellectual soulmates. Consider only if they will make good playgroup mothers. In fact, some very successful playgroups have been run by mothers who maintain quite businesslike, though not unfriendly, relations for the whole playgroup year.

A way to tell if a mother will do well with a playgroup is to consider her home. Does her household run smoothly? Is there a generally calm atmosphere about the home and family? Is the playroom pleasant and well organized? Does she handle her own children confidently and fairly? Is she generally in control of herself and her children? Is she clearly in charge and yet not too intimidating?

As for the mother personally—is she reliable? Is she reasonably patient, relaxed, mature? Most important, can she conceive of the idea that the playgroup might be fun for her as well as for the kids? A mother who thinks of her playgroup morning as an ordeal she must suffer in order to have the other three or four mornings free will pass her dislike of the playgroup on to the children.

Before you invite a mother to join you in forming a playgroup, make sure that her ideas about child-rearing and discipline are similar to yours. A strict disciplinarian will not get along well in a group of three fairly permissive mothers.

The mothers' meeting

When you have rounded up three or four mothers, you must meet to decide on basic playgroup policies and to set up schedules. It is best to have this meeting in the evening, without any children underfoot. In an informal way, one mother (usually the one at whose house the meeting is being held) can take charge and introduce the topics that ought to be discussed and decided upon. Here are eleven basic topics that ought to be discussed at your playgroup mothers' meeting:

A WEEKLY SCHEDULE

The best playgroup schedule gives each mother one regular day each week: Mother A has playgroup every Monday, Mother B every Tuesday, etc. If there are four children in the playgroup, there will be four regular playgroup days each week and one free day. Since each mother must arrange her schedule so that she will be free of all other duties on her playgroup day, it is much easier to see that these arrangements are permanent and reliable if playgroup falls on the same day each week. It must be understood by each mother that playgroup should only be canceled when absolutely necessary—when she or her child is sick, or some family emergency comes up. If it is merely a question of convenience—guests coming for dinner that night, a one-day sale downtown, an old friend in town for the day—you can try to switch days with another mother, but even this should be done infrequently.

At first the youngest children may be unaware of the days of the week, but many children quickly learn their playgroup schedule: Monday at Julie's house, Tuesday at Michael's house . . . and they dislike changes in the routine. After a few weeks of playgroup you may find your child starting off each day by asking, "What day is it, Mommy?" and then announcing proudly, "Oh, playgroup at Suzie's today."

Other systems are possible. A playgroup with three or four children can be held every day, or a playgroup with five children can be held three days a week. Each mother must then get a copy of a monthly schedule, and must make sure each week that other arrangements are made for her other children.

HOURS

A period of two and a half hours with lunch included is probably as long as you would want to be in charge of a group of children. Mothers running a playgroup for the first time are often surprised at how long an hour indoors with four small children can seem, especially during the more difficult first weeks of playgroup. It is for this reason that it is recommended that you make lunch a part of your playgroup morning. Eating is a sure-fire amusement. Four or five children usually have a great time at lunch together, as long as a minimal amount of discipline is maintained. You can prepare a simple lunch of soup, a sandwich, milk and a dixie cup in a few minutes, or in advance. That leaves only two hours to plan for, and if that period is broken up with a snack and a brief outing, the period of indoor activities will not loom so large. A schedule that has been found to work successfully begins the playgroup morning at 10 A.M. and ends after lunch at 12:30. This gives you plenty of time to get your child dressed and ready in the morning, and gets him home in time for a 1 P.M. nap, if he still naps. You might try this schedule for a few weeks. Then, if you or some of the other mothers find it too long, you can all decide to shorten the playgroup morning by half an hour. If, on the other hand, you are all having a perfectly delightful, easy time of it, you can try adding a half an hour to the playgroup morning by starting at 9:30.

GETTING TO AND FROM PLAYGROUP

In most playgroups each child is dropped off at the home where the group is meeting and picked up there at the end of the morning. Some playgroups have worked out other arrangements: The mother in charge picks up each child at his house, making the rounds with her own child. Then, with the whole group gathered outside, the morning can begin with outdoor play. After forty-five minutes or an hour she takes the group to her house for indoor activities and lunch. After lunch each child is called for by a grownup.

Another method is to have each child dropped off at playgroup by a grownup. After indoor activities and a snack, the group goes outdoors to play. Then the whole group makes the rounds, dropping a child off at each house until just the mother in charge and her own child are left.

These systems become difficult and complicated when the weather is bad, or when the children do not live very near to each other. Having each child dropped off and called for by a grownup is the simplest system.

A DAILY ROUTINE

It is good to establish a basic routine which all the mothers agree to follow for each playgroup morning. Of course it must be flexible and may even be completely changed when the children demand their favorite activities or become absorbed in something and don't want to be interrupted. The following is a good basic schedule for a two-and-a-half hour playgroup morning. It should be used only as a loose guide, even though it states specific times for specific things.

10–10:40–free play (in an organized play area, with art materials available)
10:40–10:50–cleanup
10:50–11–snack
11–11:45–if weather permits, an outing to the park, playground or just outside the house to blow soap bubbles. Indoors, this is the time for group activities: marching, singing games, simple running games, storytelling
11:45–11:55–cleanup and washing up for lunch
11:55–12:15–lunch
12:15–12:30–free play until mothers come

MOTHERS' PARTICIPATION

A most important basic policy to agree upon is that the mother in charge must be in the playroom at all times, supervising, guiding, observing, praising. You may wish to take brief notes about the children's activities, in order to give each other an idea of what your children do at other homes. But these notes must really be simple and factual, with absolutely no psychological insights and comments. For example, Jenny: blocks, doll corner with Julie, sang all verses of "I've Been Working on the Railroad" for all children. Michael: painted; made green and orange by mixing colors, played freight train with Jonathan.

Chapter 6 discusses the mother's role in the playgroup in detail.

EQUIPMENT

You should all agree to try to organize your playrooms in the best possible ways for good play (see Chapter 4). Art materials —paints, clay, collage stuff—should be available in each playroom and made ready for the children before they arrive. Each house should have smocks, scissors and paintbrushes for each child, or else each child can bring a playgroup bag containing these items with him each day. Blocks ought to be available in at least two playgroup homes. These can be made or bought communally. From now on, you ought to buy toys with the playgroup in mind. When Christmas or birthdays come around, you can suggest gift ideas to relatives and friends that can be useful for playgroup—puzzles, art equipment, records, books.

BATHROOM HABITS

If there are any particular problems in this area, you ought to bring them up at this meeting. Each mother should tell the others her general policies, whether her child needs reminding to go to the bathroom, or if he waits until the last possible moment and then makes a mad dash. You should find out if all the children wear approximately the same sizes, so that they can borrow each other's clothes in case of accidents. If any child is likely to have accidents he ought to have extra clothes at the homes of any of the other children whose clothes he can't possibly wear. A casual, matter-of-fact attitude should be adopted about going to the bathroom and, of course, a sympathetic, friendly treatment of accidents. Accidents are cut down when all mothers make sure that their children go to the bathroom before playgroup. It might be added that not infrequently, toilet-training problems that have gone on this long are quickly solved in the course of a playgroup where the child may observe, perhaps for the first time, other children of his own age going to the bathroom without any problems. Playgroup may also be the first occasion that sex differences are noticed by some of the children. Here too a matter-of-fact, unembarrassed explanation by the mother in charge is important. Curiosity about sex differences is normal at this age and should not be hushed up or discouraged.

CLOTHES

The children should wear simple, washable playclothes at all times. They should be encouraged to take off and put on their own outer clothes. If they don't know how to put on a jacket or sweater, this might be one of the first things to teach them when the playgroup gets going. Otherwise every outing, especially in winter, will take half the morning to get started. There is a simple, almost foolproof way to teach a young child how to put on a jacket: the jacket is spread out on the floor, back side down. The child stands behind the collar, facing it. He then stoops down, places his hands as far into the sleeves as he can, lifts the whole garment up and raises it over his head in an arc. The jacket is on. From now on when buying clothes for your child, look for things he can manage by himself. Snowsuits that zip at the ankle are easy for a small child to manage. Boots that zip or buckle are preferable to the slip-on kind.

FOOD

If lunch is to be included in the playgroup morning, the mothers should discuss their children's eating habits at this meeting. Be sure to mention allergies and particular likes and dislikes. It is good to know which child always eats like a bird and which has a ravenous appetite. The mother of a hearty eater might worry about a child who eats only a quarter of a sandwich and a glass of milk, unless warned in advance that this is that child's usual lunch. If any child has a specific dislike, his mother might mention it and the other mothers can try not to serve it at playgroup lunch. However, if a whole class of foods, such as vegetables, is disliked by a certain child, these should still be served, and some casually placed on his plate each time. He should not be coaxed to eat vegetables, but often the sight of his playgroup friends eating and enjoying some food will lead him to try it and find that he likes it. He may still refuse it at home, but his mother will be interested (and chagrined) to discover that he eats it with great pleasure at playgroup.

One important rule should be established for mealtime: absolutely no horseplay, throwing of food, bubbling of milk and so on. If a firm stand is taken at the first sign of trouble, the children will probably drop it altogether.

Mealtime can be one of the most completely enjoyable times of the playgroup morning. Eating is still a major source of pleasure for most three- and four-year-olds and this, combined with their natural burgeoning social instincts, makes having lunch together a lot of fun. For this reason you should limit the emphasis on good behavior, polite table manners, posture, or even nutrition at these occasions. Sit back and let the kids have fun, drawing the line, of course, at any horseplay. Some mothers make a rule that the children must stay at the table until the meal is over. This may work out well in many cases, especially if the mother has supplied the table with picture cards or books or some small toys to keep them amused. If one child is a much slower eater than the others, however, it is difficult to keep the others waiting for their dessert; on the other hand, it is unfair to hurry the deliberate eater. In such cases, you might let the children leave the table and call them back for dessert. Since you do not want them to be unsupervised for any long period of time, you might suggest that each bring a toy back to the kitchen. You could play a game or read a story to them at the table until the slow child is ready or simply have a conversation about something that might interest them.

You should agree on a policy about candy, lollipops, gum and other sweets. The recommended policy: none at all at playgroup. Children of this age are not casual about goodies. A lollipop can completely engross a three-year-old for fifteen minutes, making any other activity impossible for him. If only for this reason, ignoring the dental case against sweets for young children, it is a good idea to agree on a no-candy policy.

DISCIPLINE

Some mothers who deal firmly and justly with their own children's misbehavior hesitate to discipline other people's children. All the mothers should agree not to be afraid to be firm with each other's children, when necessary. At the start of playgroup, each mother should explain clearly the rules of the house to the children: which rooms are out of bounds, where, if anywhere, they may ride tricycles or go-carts, rules about grabbing, sharing, putting away toys, ball-playing, toy-throwing, etc. Then she should stick to her rules. Children like to know the limits of their freedom, even if they occasionally forget or ignore or challenge them. They feel secure in the knowledge that they are being taken care of, that they will not be allowed to misbehave too badly and that they can concentrate happily on their play rather than having to make any decisions about how to behave.

HEALTH

A policy must be set about colds. Many playgroups reach the doldrums in winter and early spring when one child after another, or perhaps all the children at once, are absent because of colds. Since virtually all children suffer colds at some time during each winter, and since the last cold symptoms may take weeks to disappear, you might consider a modified policy towards colds: children with fresh colds must stay home; but after two or three days, if the child is otherwise healthy and the only symptoms are a slightly runny nose and a small cough, it is probably all right to send him to playgroup. If the weather is bitterly cold or windy or otherwise unpleasant, the playgroup might skip its morning outing if someone has just come back after a bout with a cold. If your child is sick on your own playgroup day, try to switch with another mother so that the other children are not disappointed at having playgroup canceled altogether.

The mothers should consider that the health of three or four other children is at stake when they send a sick child to playgroup. Therefore, if your child seems somewhat out of sorts on a playgroup morning, take his temperature before sending him on to playgroup. Even if his temperature is normal, follow your

instincts and consider keeping him home just in case. After three
or four years, most mothers have acquired pretty reliable instincts
about when their children are coming down with something. Of
course if any of the children have been exposed to a communi-
cable disease, a doctor must be consulted as to incubation
period before the child is sent to playgroup.

If any children have particular medical problems or need
regular medication, a pediatrician ought to be consulted before
starting the child in a playgroup. These problems must be
brought up at this meeting and explicit directions in writing
as to medication and what to do in an emergency must be
supplied to each of the other mothers.

Each playgroup mother should post near her telephone the
following emergency numbers: a pediatrician, police and fire
departments, poison-control center, if there is one in the community, and one or two neighbors she can call on in an emergency.
Each mother should supply each other mother with an emergency number to call in case she cannot be reached at a particular time. The father's work number is best for this purpose,
if he can be reached easily by phone. Otherwise, give a grand-
parent's number or a close friend's. All these precautions may
seem unnecessary—and they almost always are. They are not
difficult to take however, and could make a tremendous difference
in a sudden emergency.

ADDITIONAL MOTHERS' MEETINGS

If everything goes well, there is no need for any additional
formal meetings of all the playgroup mothers. Small problems
can be ironed out on the telephone or when you pick up your
child at the end of playgroup. (Not at the beginning of the
morning, however, when the mother in charge is most occupied
with the children.)

Some problems and dilemmas are serious enough to call for
another mothers' meeting. If one of the mothers cannot cope
with a certain child or if one or more of the mothers feel a
certain child is having a destructive impact on the other children
in the group, a meeting should be held and the problem discussed among all the mothers. Perhaps one of the mothers can

help with some suggestions of how she manages to cope with a certain child. Or the mothers might decide on a consistent policy to use with a certain child: more firmness or more direction in his activities. When there are serious difficulties, a time limit can be decided upon, after which, if no improvement has been shown, the child will have to leave the playgroup. It is a mistake to disband the whole playgroup because of difficulties with one child. If all the mothers have made an honest effort to work with him and have not succeeded, they owe it to the other children in the group to have the difficult child leave the group. The mother of a difficult child can hardly be unaware of his problems and will usually understand why he is being asked to leave.

If a new child enters the group later than the others, another mothers' meeting should be held to indoctrinate the new mother on the basic policies of the playgroup and to discuss how best to introduce the newcomer into the group.

At the end of a successful playgroup year it can be most valuable and enlightening to hold a final mothers' meeting to discuss what the playgroup has meant to the mothers and the children and what special insights each mother can offer about the other children.

CHAPTER 4

The Playroom

The importance of a well-planned playroom

THE arrangement of the playroom and the organization of play materials directly influence how the children play and what they learn. A room where everything is stored out of their reach and where neatness and the mother's convenience are most important is likely to result in unimaginative or apathetic play. On the other hand, a room that is cluttered and disorganized, where anything goes anywhere, where puzzles have pieces missing, books are torn and records are cracked—is almost certain to bring about chaotic, unproductive and possibly destructive play. A good playroom lies somewhere between these two extremes. It will be carefully organized to invite the children's interest; things will belong in certain places where they can always find them and get them without help; the arrangement of the room should encourage them to play together and learn from each other, one of the primary goals of any playgroup.

You do not need expensive equipment for your playroom. You probably already have many of the materials you need and in Part Two you will find suggestions for improvising play materials out of things at hand or things you can get at little or no cost. Whatever you need to buy will probably be used by your children playing alone, as well as by the playgroup.

Basic equipment

A WORKTABLE AND CHAIRS

A low worktable, at which all the children can sit and work together, and a child-sized chair or stool for each child is indispensable for any playgroup. The children become a real group around the worktable, making collages, molding clay, making cotton-swab paintings, having a snack—and all the while talking, observing each other's work, and enjoying being together. Each child can make a collage or play with clay by himself, at home; doing these things at a table with three other children becomes a whole new experience and this is the essence of the playgroup idea.

The worktable should be 20″ to 24″ in height and have about 36″ x 24″ in surface area; the chairs should be 10″ to 14″ high. A circular table should be at least 30″ in diameter. A good children's table can be bought but it is quite expensive. A perfectly good worktable for children can be obtained by buying a second-hand kitchen or dining-room table (the old-fashioned kind with an enamel top is wonderful) and simply cutting the legs down a few inches to make it the right height for the children's chairs. Or you may make a table very easily from scratch by buying a sturdy piece of wood of the right size and attaching ready made legs to it. You can cover the top with linoleum, formica or self-sticking adhesive, to make cleaning up easier.

STORAGE SPACE

Art materials, blocks and other toys should be stored on low shelves where the children can see them and take them out by themselves. This idea sounds frightening to some mothers—"Oh, they'll just pull everything off the shelves and make a horrible mess!"—but this need not happen if a rule about taking out one thing at a time is clearly established at the outset, and if the supervising mother helps the children put things away when they're finished. By allowing them the freedom to choose what they want to do during the free-play period and making it possible for them to get at materials without your help, you are encouraging them to be independent, to make choices and decisions for themselves.

Open bookcases or cabinets can be bought for very little at department stores, unpainted furniture centers or second-hand furniture stores. Of course the size depends on the space available in your playroom, but the shelves should be low enough for a child to reach and fairly deep (very narrow bookcases are not practical).

A teacart is a good substitute for a storage shelf, especially for art materials, and has the advantage of being movable.

You can make your own storage shelves quite easily out of planks and dowels or, if you have sturdy walls, you can attach shelves to brackets on the wall.

A low-cost substitute for storage shelves can be made from commercial wooden milk crates, which you can buy at your grocery store for about twenty-five cents. Four of these bolted together make a perfectly fine block case or bookcase. If you paint them in bright colors and top them with a plank of wood or plywood covered with linoleum or self-sticking paper, they lose their makeshift look and become attractive pieces of furniture.

Of course toys and materials should be organized in boxes and containers on the shelves, not merely thrown in haphazardly. The best organizing container for large collections of toys such as wooden trains or alphabet blocks is the heavy cardboard carton that quart-sized beer bottles come in. You can get these at your supermarket for about thirty-five cents. They are reinforced with metal at the sides and this makes them virtually indestructible. For smaller toys you can use cigar boxes, shoe boxes, cannisters, coffee tins with plastic lids, gift boxes—almost anything. Your playroom will look more cheerful if you paint the cardboard boxes and cover the coffee tins with bright self-sticking paper.

A PORTABLE PHONOGRAPH AND SELECTED RECORDS

A good portable phonograph can be bought for about fifteen dollars and is worth its weight in gold to you and your playgroup.

For quiet listening, marching, dancing, activity songs and singing games, you will find the phonograph the most versatile and useful piece of equipment in your playroom. If you have a hi-fi in your living room you can use that instead, but it brings the playgroup out of the playroom and deprives the children of the fun of putting the records on themselves. A piano can substitute for a phonograph, if you play reasonably well and if you don't mind the children marching, dancing, running and jumping in the room where the piano is located.

A good selection of records is important and you will find a recommended list at the end of Chapter 8. You don't need many; five carefully selected records will serve your purposes very well.

AN EASEL

Children *can* paint at the worktable, or even on the floor, and if your playroom is large enough to set aside an area for painting on the floor or if you have room for *two* worktables, one of which can be a painting table, then you can do without an easel. But if your space is limited, an easel is the most convenient and space-saving arrangement for painting, well worth the investment query. There are suggestions for substitutes in the painting section of Chapter 7.

BLOCKS AND ACCESSORIES

A good set of wooden blocks of varying shapes and sizes is a good investment for your playgroup, and for your family, too. Blocks offer endless opportunities for imaginative play, encourage social play, and their educational value is well known. There are also interlocking heavy cardboard "building boards," and reinforced cardboard blocks for a different kind of block play. Chapter 12 gives suggestions for the kinds of blocks to get and also some do-it-yourself ideas.

ART MATERIALS

The art materials you should have include poster paints of different colors, brushes, clay, paste—these need to be bought, preferably in large quantities before your first playgroup meeting —and a good collection of junk for making collages, mobiles and stabiles. Other suggested art materials can be found in Chapter 7.

MUSIC MATERIALS

A good collection of rhythm instruments—either manufactured ones such as drums, tambourines, maracas, bells, triangles and cymbals, or improvised ones such as coffee-can drums, pots and pans, tea balls (see Chapter 8)—should be available during free-play period, and for marching and group activities.

PROPS FOR MAKE-BELIEVE PLAY

By digging through your old things, borrowing or swapping, you can accumulate a collection of clothes, toys and junk that the children can use as props for make-believe play. Ask your neighbors and friends if you might look through the toys their children have outgrown before they throw them out or give them away and see what you can glean for your playgroup. Try to collect as many similar toys as you can: two or three toy telephones inspire many imaginary conversations, three or four freight trains or trucks lead to games of loading and unloading that can take up the entire free-play period, and four friction cars or buses will lead to a great race. Collect things for a grocery store, doctor's office, shoe store and playhouse. Collect hats, jewelry, and old clothes for costumes. (See Chapter 15 for more suggestions.)

BOOKS

Storytime is one of the easiest playgroup activities for the mother and one of the most enjoyable for the children. You will not need a great many storybooks; you will find that the children demand their favorites time after time, but the greater number and variety of books you have, the more eager they will become to hear more books and eventually read books for themselves. See Chapter 10 for a discussion of how to choose books for preschoolers and a list of suggested books. There is no reason for you to buy books, however, if you wish to use library books. The children can also bring their favorites for the group to hear.

Optional equipment

A LARGE BULLETIN BOARD

A bulletin board hung at a child's eye-level can be used to display the children's art work and for putting up magazine pictures related to their current interests and activities. Not only does a bulletin board full of colorful pictures cheer up and decorate a playroom, but it serves an educational purpose too, if used thoughtfully by an observant mother. For instance, if the children have spent their free-play period playing a make-believe game of "airport," some pictures on the bulletin board at the next playgroup meeting of a real airport will give the children a better idea of what a real airport is like and suggest new ideas for their make-believe play and block building. A folder full of pictures clipped out of magazines is easy to accumulate and will give you many chances to augment and enrich the children's play.

A COAT RACK

A bar with four or five coat hooks or dowels hung on the back of a door will allow the children to hang up their own coats when they come in and find them again by themselves when they go out. This will save you time and is another small way of encouraging the children to do things for themselves. A children's coat rack, usually in the shape of an animal, with dowels sticking out at various levels, can be bought at many department stores.

Organizing the playroom into areas of interest

Organizing the playroom into separate areas of interest is the most effective way of encouraging free, constructive and undistracted play. Nursery school playrooms are divided into "corners" and even the smallest playgroup playroom can be organized in this way, on a smaller scale. The music area in your playroom may simply be a cardboard box with rhythm instruments and bells that sits on a certain table or shelf; the important thing is that all the music things are in one place and the children know where to find them.

THE ART AREA

If there is good natural light in the room, the art area ought to be as near the window as possible. If there is a bathroom adjoining the playroom, having the art area near it will save you many steps and much mess. The art area should include the worktable, easel and a shelf, teacart or cabinet with paper, paste, scissors, collage stuff and any other art materials. Since the children will not be pouring the paints, these can be stored in the bathroom, kitchen, or anywhere convenient for you.

THE BLOCK AREA

The block area should be in a part of the room with enough floor space for building large constructions without impeding passage to any other area of the room. The blocks should be organized according to shape and size and stored on low, open shelves. Block accessories should be stored nearby according to categories (farm animals, zoo animals, cars, etc.) in separate containers. Large, hollow blocks, reinforced cardboard building blocks and interlocking building boards can be piled neatly against the wall.

THE MAKE-BELIEVE AREA

If your child is a girl, your make-believe area is likely to take the form of a doll corner and you probably have much of the equipment already: dolls, crib or doll bed, stove and housekeeping equipment, tea-party things, doll carriage and so on. The doll corner should be arranged as much as possible like a little stage, for the play that goes on there thrives on a theatrical setting.

Mothers of boys usually don't have dolls and toy housekeeping equipment. Their make-believe area can be set up as a grocery store, doctor's office, shoe store or firehouse. You will find suggestions for make-believe play settings in Chapter 14. But all the equipment and accessories for make-believe play should be carefully organized and kept in a separate area that can be set up attractively before the children come and that they can arrange and rearrange themselves.

Setting up before the playgroup arrives

Having the playroom set up and ready when the first child arrives can make all the difference between an organized, orderly and creative free-play period and a wild and unhappy one. It affects the children's feelings about themselves and their playgroup in a subtle but definite way: if they see you have gone to the trouble of preparing things for them, they feel a sense of pride and importance and an eagerness to participate.

Start setting up the playroom half an hour before the children are due to arrive. Your own child will probably enjoy helping you. Paints, paintbrushes and water should be ready at the easel. Clay, playdough or collage materials should be set out for each child at the worktable. The make-believe area should be arranged in an inviting way. If there is a bulletin board, appropriate pictures should be pinned up. (If you are planning to bake cookies, for instance, you might put up pictures of cookies, or of the separate ingredients.) Blocks and block accessories should be ready in their special places, and music materials in theirs. Selected records should be out by the phonograph, and selected books for storytelling should be out on a table or on the bed. Don't wait to do all this until the children arrive: you will be needed for other things then. If the room is prepared for them, you will not have to coax them to play or even suggest what to do: the playroom will do it for you.

CHAPTER 5

The First Days and Before

The problems that face your child

BEFORE your child can settle down to have fun and really get something out of his playgroup, he has two difficult obstacles to overcome. First he must contend with a new world of three or four new homes, new mothers, new children and the new experience of being a member of a group. Most grownups feel a little queasy when they embark on something entirely new and unknown, and so it is easy to understand how even something as simple and cozy as a neighborhood playgroup can be an overwhelming and scarey experience to a three-year-old. Then there is the matter of leaving his mother regularly, albeit for short periods of time. This is an important step for him to take, a necessary beginning in the process of becoming an independent person.

Each child reacts differently to these problems. Some children seem to sail into new experiences without a moment's hesitation; others are more cautious and somewhat unwilling to try new things. Some children have much more trouble separating from their mothers than others. It depends a great deal upon the child's natural temperament and past experiences as well as upon the mother's handling of the separation. Of course the two problems are closely connected: as the new situation becomes more familiar, the child will probably find it easier to separate from his mother.

There are ways you can help your child get off to a good start

in his playgroup. You can make the situation less unknown and
frightening and the separation easier to manage by some advance
preparation. Introduce your child to playgroup gradually and
carefully. It's worth taking a few extra pains and starting off
well, for you may not be able to undo a bad beginning. On the
other hand, don't overdo it. If you talk, talk, talk about playgroup
and build it up into something glorious, you will certainly arouse
your child's suspicions. "Something's fishy," he is likely to think,
"why does she want so much for me to go to playgroup?" In
all your advance preparation of your child, try to be casual,
matter-of-fact and truthful.

Making the unknown more familiar

GETTING TO KNOW THE OTHER CHILDREN BEFOREHAND

If your child knows and has played with all the children in
the playgroup one by one before they meet as a group, his adjustment to playgroup will be smoother. Since the children all
live in the same neighborhood, the chances are that some of
them know each other already and have played at each other's
houses. Try to arrange to have your child play individually with
each of the children before playgroup begins officially, at your
house and at the other child's house. This will help him enormously. Playgroup will still be a new experience, but your child
will be less likely to be overwhelmed if some things are familiar
on the first day.

This also gives the mothers a chance to get to know each other
and the children who will be in their charge once a week. An
excellent plan, if you have plenty of time, is to start the playgroup in the fall, around the time school begins, and use the
summer beforehand to get acquainted with the other playgroup
mothers and children. When your child first meets a future
playgroupmate, tell him casually that soon, or in the fall, or
around the time big brother goes back to school, he will have
a playgroup in the mornings, and Helen will be one of his
playgroup friends. He will have time to get used to the idea

of playgroup, and what's more, when the inevitable grown-up question comes, "Do you go to school?" he will probably enjoy answering "I'm going to playgroup in the fall."

KNOWING WHAT TO EXPECT

Your child will be more likely to start off with good feelings about his playgroup if he has a fairly clear idea of what it is all about. A simple way to let him know what to expect is to incorporate the information about what a playgroup is and what he will be doing there into a story or a series of stories. Young children love to hear stories about themselves and their friends and familiar events. You don't have to make it sound exciting by telling about marvelous good times, trips to the zoo or parties; the everyday activities like building a house out of blocks, playing grocery store, painting or having lunch together will not sound uninteresting to your child. Include the names of the other children in the playgroup in your story and, if you have the patience for it, repeat the names of all four or five children every time they do something new in the "playgroup story." Children love repetition, and by repeating all of the names each time, you will give your child an idea of what a group is. You can prepare your child for some of the problems that will come up in playgroup by incorporating them into variations of your playgroup story—two children may fight over a toy, or one child may knock down another's tower—but the moral lesson should not be emphasized. It is not necessary to go on and on about sharing and taking turns and not grabbing from other children. You are not really trying to teach these concepts in your story—the children will learn about them from experience—you are simply preparing your child for their happening.

TELLING THE OTHER MOTHERS ABOUT YOUR CHILD

The more the other mothers know about your child and his temperament, the better they will be able to cope with any problems he may have and to help him feel at home. General information about your child—he's shy with strangers, he's bursting with energy and needs to let loose frequently, he never spends much time at one thing, he gets so absorbed in what he's doing he forgets everything else—will help the other mothers know how to deal with him. Specific information—he's afraid of animals, he doesn't like to use other people's bathrooms, he eats very slowly, he doesn't like chocolate ice-cream, he loves puzzles and can do very hard ones, he's interested in numbers, he's crazy about airplanes—can prevent troubles and misunderstandings and give the other mothers ideas about how to make your child happy.

Making separation easier to manage

THE MOTHER'S ATTITUDE

There is a definite relation between the mother's feelings about leaving her child and the child's feelings about being left. If the mother is fearful and nervous and expects trouble the child will surely sense it, no matter what jolly and cheerful words she uses. If she feels quite confident that he will have fun playing with the other children, that the other mothers will take good care of him and that he is ready to grow a little independent of her, then in most cases he will have little trouble separating from her. It is hard to legislate feelings, however, and just as every child feels a little worried about leaving his mother, so every mother has mixed feelings about leaving her child and seeing him grow less dependent upon her. It is important to convince yourself of the value to your child of joining a playgroup and the fun in store for him there, really much more fun than he would have alone at home. Remember that by three most children are ready for a short separation from their mothers, and that the ability to manage this separation brings them great satisfaction.

The mother's reasons for sending her child to playgroup make a difference in her attitude too, and in her child's adjustment. If the main idea is getting rid of the child for a while (of course everybody feels this a *little*), the child is apt to sense it and balk at being left. The mother who really believes that playgroup is a great thing for her child, that he will gain a lot from it and enjoy himself, will find it easy to convey the feeling that she is not leaving him, but rather letting *him* leave *her* because he will have a good time. This may be using "child psychology," but if you can honestly communicate this to your child it will help make the separation go more smoothly.

PREPARING YOUR CHILD FOR SEPARATION

It is best to have a definite plan for carrying out the separation and to tell your child very simply what it will be: "Today your playgroup is going to be at Janet's house and I'm going to stay there the whole time because it's the first playgroup day there. But the next time you go to playgroup at Janet's house, Helen (Janet's mother) will be the playgroup mother and I'll say goodby to you at the door." Before the next playgroup meeting, repeat the whole thing again about staying at Jenny's house, even using the same words if you wish. By the end of the week your child will have gotten the idea. You might remind him that now you have stayed at everybody's house one time and that next week the mommies will have to say goodby at the door. Sometimes it helps to establish a parting routine such as "When I say goodby at Helen's house I'll say, 'See you later, alligator,' and you'll say to me, 'In a while, crocodile.' Let's try that now." When the time comes your child may be so busy going through the routine, he will hardly notice that you've gone.

The first moments of separation are invariably the hardest. In many cases the tears and entreaties at leaving time are used to get at *you* and test your confidence. But if you're already out the door, most children are realistic enough to know that there is nothing much they can do. Pretty soon they will be having so much fun that next time they will feel even less reluctant to have you leave.

A MORE GRADUAL SEPARATION FOR SOME CHILDREN

Staying at playgroup without their mothers after a week works well for most children. But a few children, for various reasons, really need to have their mothers stay longer. Their panic and fear at the idea of mommy leaving are unmistakably genuine. In these cases, a more gradual separation is called for. Instead of a week the separation process may take a month or more, and this requires patience and understanding from all the play-group mothers.

For the first few times, you might find some inconspicuous corner of the playroom to sit in, with a book to keep you occupied. Don't insist that your child go play with the other children or take part in the activities that are available. Let him stand at your side or even sit on your lap for a while if he wants to. You can be absolutely sure that he will become interested in what the other children are doing and want to participate—it's just a question of time. The mother in charge will probably try to include him in some of the activities, or the other children may become interested in getting him to join them. He will begin to become interested in other things and leave you for short periods.

As soon as he feels more confident, you can try to leave the room for a little while. Don't sneak out, but don't reveal your anxiety by asking him if he will allow you to leave the room. When he is happily playing with a toy or doing a puzzle, an-nounce loudly to the mother in charge that you are terribly thirsty and are going to the kitchen for a glass of water. Without looking at your child for his reaction (you'll hear from him if he is alarmed), leave the room slowly. He can come with you if he is upset. The odds are he won't. Don't stay out of the room too long the first time.

As soon as you see that he is spending more time playing than standing at your side, tell him on your way to playgroup that you think you'll stay in the living room for the morning because the chair is more comfortable there.

When he is quite adjusted to having you in another room for the whole morning and hardly ever comes to check on you, you can start working on leaving the house, for short periods at first and finally for the whole morning. After your child has settled down at some activity, come into the playroom and ask the mother in charge a pre-arranged question—does she have a pack of cigarettes or the morning newspaper—and when she answers no, tell your child that you have to go to the drugstore and that you'll be back in a few minutes. Be sure you don't ask him if it's all right with him for you to leave—tell him. When this has been carried off successfully, there is every indication that your child is ready to be left for the whole morning.

THE MOTHER IN CHARGE CAN HELP

When a child in your playgroup needs his mother to stay with him longer than the first week, you can help both the child and his mother work out their problem successfully. It is easy to be critical of another mother's handling of her child, especially when your own child has had no trouble at all adjusting to playgroup. You may feel that the other mother is "babying" her child too much, that he would do just fine if she simply marched out and didn't worry about him so much. But if a mother has decided that her child needs a more gradual separation, it is important for the other mothers to cooperate with her. If your playgroup is to run smoothly, it is important to maintain a sympathetic, uncritical attitude towards the other mothers and often you may find that another mother's way, while different from yours, works for her own child.

When one of the children is clinging to his mother and not joining any of the activities, you should try casually and cheerfully to interest him in something, fully prepared for a refusal. If you are distributing rhythm instruments, for instance, you might go up to him and let him pick out an instrument, telling him that if he doesn't want to join the others on the rug he can bang on the tambourine right where he is and they'll all hear him. Or you might gather the children together for a story near enough to the outsider to pique his curiosity. More often than not, he will move a little closer to the group without even knowing it, and this may be the beginning of a successful separation for him.

Delayed reactions and later separation problems

It often happens that a child who has adjusted to separation very quickly and cheerfully has a delayed reaction a few weeks or even months later. This is always puzzling and worrisome for the child's mother. Why does her child suddenly cling to her at the door and not want her to leave? Worse still, why does he say "I don't *want* to go to playgroup," and refuse to get dressed in the morning, when he seemed so enthusiastic at the start? Usually the answer is not that something is going wrong with the playgroup. Often the child is testing, to see what mommy will say and do and to find out just how she feels about his playgroup. Also, some of the newness and excitement have worn off by now and the child suddenly realizes that he has given something up in exchange for his good time at playgroup: time with mommy. He may be feeling a momentary pang of regret for his not-too-remote babyhood.

What is the best way to handle these situations? If a child says, "I don't want to go to playgroup," insisting that he *has* to go may serve to make him feel more stubborn and resistant, and may change his good feelings about playgroup into resentment. On the other hand, hesitation and uncertainty on your part— "Why don't you want to go? Don't you like playgroup?"—is asking him to make the decision that he really wants *you* to make for him. Moreover, if you don't seem too sure that playgroup is the right place for him to go every morning, he is bound to sense this and really begin to fight going. It is best to accept his reluctance and resistance with sympathy, while maintaining a feeling of certainty about his attendance at playgroup. You might tell him about some occasions when *you* hadn't wanted to do something and had just felt like staying home. You can tell him that joining a playgroup means going every time, that the other children would miss him if he didn't come, that he really *is* important to the group. If you continue to feel confident about the playgroup and its value to your child, you will find it easy to keep an air of inevitability about his attendance. Many children need some face-saving "out" when they have said they won't do something before they will reverse their position. Almost any change in the routine might serve as an "out"—having Daddy take him to playgroup instead of you, or taking his tricycle along, or even giving him a ride to playgroup in the baby's stroller. If your child is quite adamant, however, and an out-and-out fight is brewing, it is better to let him stay home and to try not to be angry at him.

If he clings to you at the door, crying that he wants you to stay with him, after having parted cheerfully for weeks, remember that growing up is not an uninterrupted process, and you can be sure that your child's anxiety about leaving you is temporary. Stay if you can, for part of the morning or for the whole session, and suggest that next time you won't be able to. Tell him that playgroup is only for children, not for mommies, and he may even begin to feel sorry for you.

In all cases of delayed reaction to playgroup, it is a good idea to try to spend some extra time alone with the child at other times, especially if there is a baby at home or older children taking up much of your attention.

The first days

The actual first day of playgroup at each house is most important to the success of the whole enterprise. If all goes smoothly and the children (and mothers) have a good time, they will all be off to a good start and look forward to the next meeting.

AN ABBREVIATED SCHEDULE

It is helpful to keep the first meetings of playgroup shorter than the regular session, perhaps no longer than an hour. This makes it easier for the other mothers who are staying for the whole session during the first week, easier for the mother in charge who is inexperienced at this sort of thing and a little unsure of herself, and for the children, who may be easily tired out by the excitement of the new situation. This makes it sensible to wait for two weeks before starting in on a full schedule. By then the children have settled down and begun to form a real group and the whole playgroup runs much more smoothly than at the beginning.

ACTIVITIES FOR THE FIRST DAY

The first day is always one of the hardest. The children have a lot to learn about getting along in a group, about sharing and taking turns and playing together in a peaceful way. The equipment is new to some of the children. The art activities may need introduction. The home child feels a natural impulse to protect his possessions, no matter how well he has been prepared for the necessity of sharing, and his behavior may be at its worst. To make things harder, the other mothers are all somewhere within earshot, causing the mother in charge to feel a natural impulse to keep peace at any price, so that they will think she is doing a good job.

It is therefore especially important to have the first day carefully planned and to have everything set up before the children arrive. There should not be a great variety of equipment out on the first day. Many new toys tend to lead to confusion and chaos. A few basic, simple activities should be available for the children: collage materials on the worktable, paints at the easel, blocks and some accessories in the block corner, a few easy puzzles and bright picture books on an open shelf. Everything else should be put away temporarily, if at all possible. Since the morning will be short, these activities should suffice to keep the children busy for a short free-play period. Then it will be snacktime, an activity that can hardly fail. After the snack, the best group activity for the first day is the one that requires the least participation from the children: a carefully chosen story. Since listening to stories is a favorite activity for young children at home, having a story at playgroup, perhaps even a story they all know already, helps them feel at home. But remember that listening to a story in a group is still a new experience, different from listening at home, so keep it short and don't feel annoyed if some of the children drift away to other activities. If the children are still eager to play after the story, you can let them have another brief free-play period and end the morning with a goodby song.

As you plan the first day, and during the actual time the children are at your house, keep in mind the goals you are trying to accomplish:

1. To establish a regular routine that the children will be able to depend upon and that will help them feel secure about playgroup. Any simple rituals you wish to repeat each time—a good-morning song or a snacktime nonsense poem—are a good idea. Even though

the morning may only be an hour, stick to the same routine you plan to maintain on your regular schedule: free play, snack, group activity. Lunch may be skipped until the regular schedule is adopted.

2. To make sure that the children have a good time and want to come back for more. Don't try to organize complicated group activities or games. Stick to the surefire favorites: simple art activities, storytelling, a snack and perhaps some very simple songs or fingerplays that they are likely to know already, such as "Eency Weency Spider."

3. To establish yourself as a friendly, protective, fair person the children can depend upon and trust. Stay calm, talk slowly and clearly, don't stint on affection if it seems called for, and most of all, try to understand the limited experience all the children have had in social relations. Hitting another child may seem to you a very unlikely way to make friends. But a three-year-old is learning the rules in the only way he knows how: trying out all the possibilities. This can account for much of the behavior that grownups automatically regard as "bad."

CHAPTER 6

Your Playgroup Morning

Supervising young children

PLANNING AHEAD

IT is often helpful to jot down a plan for the playgroup morning, checking to make sure that everything is ready before the children arrive. The plan should include what art equipment you will set up for the free-play period, what your make-believe corner will be, what the snack will be, what outing or group activity you will try, what story you will read, what songs, what games. Of course any plan will be useful only as a rough guide, and you may want to change in midstream, if the children get involved with something else, or are getting tired, or if the activity you have planned isn't successful. It is important to take the children's lead, and to be flexible. But having a plan to follow (or to deviate from) helps you stay in control of any situation and avoids confusion and possible disappointment.

TIMING

Every playgroup morning requires careful timing. Young children have a short attention span and tire easily. Therefore, in planning your morning, you should include changes of tempo as well as changes of activities; active play should be alternated with periods of quiet and restful activities.

It is up to the mother in charge to be sensitive to the children's behavior and know when it is time to change the tempo. Often falling down, dropping or spilling things, or generally undesirable social behavior is a sign of fatigue and an indication that it is time for a quiet activity, such as storytelling, singing, fingerplays. Letting-off-steam activities include running and skipping to music, punching a punchball, woodwork, and singing games.

ALLOWING PLENTY OF TIME

It is important to allow plenty of time for all activities to avoid the necessity of hurrying four young children. Every mother knows the annoyance and chagrin of being in a hurry with a small child in tow. The child seems to move slower and slower in direct proportion to her hurry. Tempers snap and both mother and child end up feeling mad and then sorry. If speed is necessary because of a special activity—a trip to the museum or firehouse—it sometimes seems that the whole trip is somewhat spoiled. It might have been a nicer morning for everyone if they had stayed at home and made collages.

For this reason, be sure that your plans take into consideration the leisurely tempo young children prefer. Don't organize your morning in such an inflexible way that you find yourself rushing from one activity to the next. If you are planning a trip, allow plenty of time for dawdling, stopping and looking.

Allow plenty of time, too, for picking up toys and washing up before lunch. These activities can be fun for the children instead of unpleasant chores, if they have enough time to do them their own way. A child may enjoy taking fifty blocks back to the block shelf one at a time, but if the mother in charge is in a hurry, this can be infuriating.

TRANSITIONS

Since going from one activity to another is not hard for grown-ups, many mothers forget that children can find transitions very hard to manage. Warning the children in advance that an activity is going to end soon, or a new activity is going to begin, will help them make the transition more easily. For instance, if two children are building a barn out of blocks and it is getting late, you might say, "You'd better get all the animals into the barn for lunch and then it will be time to put the blocks away so we can get ready for *our* lunch," or "We'll sing one last song and then we'll put on our coats to go out to the park and blow soap bubbles."

Some children cope with transitions better than others. When you are changing activities, try to start with the easygoing child who usually cooperates, and often the other children will follow his example. And be ingenious; a song or a simple story will often bridge two activities smoothly.

PREVENTING TROUBLE BEFORE IT BEGINS

It might be said that a playgroup functions well because of the things that *don't* happen.

The mother in charge must be alert for signs of trouble and should step in to prevent it. This does not mean that she must solve every problem or help the children at the slightest difficulty: on the contrary, the problems the children are capable of solving by themselves are most valuable to them as a means of learning. But she must be sensitive to signs of trouble beyond the capabilities of the children. She need not step in the moment a child has difficulty doing a puzzle; if he cannot find the right pieces but is earnestly, thoughtfully trying to work it out, the mother should give him a chance to do it himself. But if she observes that he is getting all worked up, that the pieces keep coming apart and he is about to smash the whole puzzle to the floor, then she should certainly go over and give him some help. Then she might direct him to a more relaxing activity that does not require such small-muscle coordination, such as fingerpainting or clay molding. If two children are playing house and a third child wants to join them, the mother in charge can prevent bad feelings by giving the third child a new accessory to bring to the game, or suggesting a role for him to play, thus bettering his chances of being accepted in the game and avoiding the hurt feelings of being rejected.

Talking to young children

YOUR VOICE

Much of the atmosphere of your playgroup morning depends upon how you talk to children. A soft, slow, soothing voice, especially when excitement is running high, helps keep a calm atmosphere in the room. Shouting at a child from across the room may have a bad effect on all the children; it is far better to take the trouble to go up to the child and tell him your message quietly.

In general, try to talk in a natural, matter-of-fact tone of voice to your playgroup children. This is hard for many grownups to achieve. But children react against a condescending, "cute" manner of talking, and are less likely to behave in a natural way if you talk unnaturally.

WHAT YOU SAY

If you talk too much to children of playgroup age, they may get into the habit of not listening to anything you say. It is better to keep your talking to a minimum. When you have something to say, remember to use simple words and phrases. Even the most complicated concepts can often be reduced to a few basic words that a three-year-old can understand.

Avoid long explanations, rationalizations, and especially avoid moralizing to young children. Don't say, "It's very naughty to hit other children. You have to try to think of how other people feel." A three-year-old couldn't care less. You might simply say, "You may not hit another child. That hurts him." By the same token, don't moralize about good behavior either: "What a good boy you are for putting all your blocks away. I bet your mommy will be proud when I tell her." It is better to simply say, "Thank you for helping."

GET HIS ATTENTION

It seems too obvious to suggest that you be sure you have the child's attention before talking to him, but many grownups talk on and on to young children without noticing whether they are really listening. This may be partly because the grownup is much taller than the child and cannot really see the child's face when talking to him. Try to sit or kneel when talking to a child so that your face is at his level, and use his name in addressing him.

USING POSITIVE WORDS

During the course of any playgroup morning, much of your talk will involve prohibiting certain activities. If possible, try to phrase these prohibitions in a positive way: say, "Try to paint on the paper," instead of "Don't paint on the easel," or "Use your fork for your meat," instead of "Don't eat with your fingers." This is elementary child psychology and it really works. Saying "don't do this" often brings out a stubborn streak in preschoolers.

Discipline and behavior problems

BASIC RULES OF CONDUCT

Every playgroup mother needs to set up a few basic rules of conduct for her playgroup morning and then try to see that the children stick to them. Most of these rules work two ways: while they prevent the child from doing something undesirable, at the same time they protect him from having something unpleasant done to him by another child. Children are quick to realize that these rules work to their advantage and are almost always willing to try to observe a few basic ones. Of course, if you set up a great many rules—about politeness and cleanliness and correct speech and habits you may consider unpleasant, such as thumb-sucking—the children are likely to balk not only at the less important rules, but at the basic ones, too. The following are the basic rules commonly set up in nursery playgroups:

Sharing: all toys that are out belong to all the children during the course of a playgroup morning. The child who has a toy first may use it until he is ready to relinquish it.

Grabbing: grabbing is not allowed. If a child wants a toy that another child is playing with, he must ask for it.

Hurting others: no child may kick, bite, hit, punch, slap or in any way hurt another child or the mother in charge. (In some cases, you might remind the children that feelings can be hurt too.)

Destructive behavior: no child may destroy another child's art work or knock down another's block structure, or interfere with the other children's play in a destructive or disruptive way.

Putting things away: the children may not drag out one toy after another. Each toy must be put away (with the mother's help, if necessary) before another can be taken down. All the children are expected to help clean up the playroom at the end of the playgroup morning.

When children misbehave

When one child is disrupting the whole group, being destructive, interfering with the other children's play, the playgroup mother must do something, for the good of all the children including the one who is misbehaving.

TRY TO FIND OUT WHY HE IS MISBEHAVING

Sometimes it is clear that a child is testing you, just to find out what you will do. In this case you will do best to be quite firm and no-nonsense about your insistence that he stop misbehaving. Sometimes he feels hurt and insecure and needs a little extra attention and affection. Try to give him the extra attention, if you can, and he may begin to play happily with the others. Sometimes you haven't the faintest idea why a child is misbehaving, and you feel yourself getting angry at him. If you have any tried and true system for keeping calm—counting to ten or reciting "The Raven"—do it. Your anger will upset all the children and will only prolong the whole episode.

TRY TO REDIRECT HIS ENERGIES

Sometimes you can solve a behavior problem by getting the child involved in another activity that interests him and calms him down at the same time. Many nursery-school teachers rely upon the soothing influence of water play to help some of their disruptive children settle down. If you are reading a story to the group and one child persists in banging the drum or singing loudly and distracting the other children, try setting him to work with a pot of water and a sponge to clean the work table. Most children love this job, calm down fairly quickly, and get a good feeling of helping and doing something worthwhile. Other jobs can have the same effect: if a child is knocking down blocks and throwing them around, you might try giving him a sanding block and letting him sand the rough edges of the blocks.

SEPARATION AS A LAST RESORT

Sometimes nothing works to make a child stop misbehaving. Then you will probably have to separate the child from the group for a while. You might say, "I cannot let you knock down everybody else's block houses. If you feel so mad just now that you can't stop doing that, you'll have to sit in the hall for a while until you feel ready to come back." Then firmly lead the child out of the room, keeping him in sight, however, when you go back inside. You might have a special corner of the playroom, or even a certain chair, where you can have a child sit until he is ready to rejoin the group.

It is important the child does not feel that this is a punishment. You might spend a few minutes with him there, just talking, or give him something to play with. Some children will come back to the group by themselves after a short while; others may need a little help from you to come back without losing face. You might go and ask him in a friendly way if he's ready to come back yet because you need him for a game, and if he's not, tell him to call or whistle for you when he is.

HE NEEDS TO BE REASSURED

When you must discipline a child, either with words or by separation from the group, try to let him feel that you disapprove of his actions, but not of him. Avoid words such as "bad boy." And let him know in some way, a hug or a warm smile will do, that even though you cannot let him behave in an unacceptable way, you still like him.

HANDLING FIGHTS

All young children fight sometimes and this is bound to be one of the most common behavior problems of any playgroup. You have established rules about sharing and not grabbing, but when two children are pulling on a toy and shrieking at each other, it is not the time to try to talk reasonably to them, explaining your rules. The first, and often most difficult, thing you must do is to calm them down and get their attention. You will not accomplish this by trying to outshout them or getting angry at them. This might make them even more upset. Try taking them each by the hand, while they are shrieking, if need be, and leading them over to the sofa or bed. Sit them each down on it, sit down between them, and say quietly, "Now, what's the trouble. What's all this fighting?" By this time they have lost some of the fire of their fight and are curious about what you are going to do. Now you can quietly and calmly explain the rules of the playgroup. A touch of humor at this point always helps divert the children and change the mood.

AVOID PLACING BLAME

When an accident has happened while you were not watching, it won't help in any way to try to find out whose fault it really was. The lamp has been broken or the milk spilled, and finding out who did it will not make it any better. It only increases the bad feelings all around, encourages the guilty child to lie and defend himself in any way he can and makes talebearers out of the other children. Most children, if not afraid of punishment, will voluntarily tell you that they did it.

AVOID BRIBES

A good reason to avoid bribery to get a child to behave the way you want is that it really doesn't work well after a while. You may find yourself in the humiliating position of offering bribe after bribe, only to be rejected by a clever little playgrouper who is waiting for something better to be offered.

The home child

The home child presents special problems for almost all playgroups. Especially at the beginning, many mothers find that their own child is most difficult to handle when the playgroup meets at their house. For the first few meetings in his own playroom the home child may be at his very worst, defending his every possession from the other children, whining, sulking, having a temper tantrum for no good reason and driving his mother wild. She is likely to become dubious about the whole idea of a playgroup. It will help her weather the difficult first weeks if she knows that he is behaving normally and typically and is sure to settle down after the first few times. There are, however, a few ways a mother can help make the initial adjustment a little easier for her child.

EXTRA ATTENTION

Part of the reason your child is difficult the first few times the playgroup meets at your house is because of the close emotional ties between you and him: he does not want to be just another member of a group to you—he wants to be special. However, you cannot give him special favors during the playgroup morning, as you must divide your attention among all the children. Still, you can try to give him a little extra attention, at other times of the day, too, during the first few weeks of playgroup, and try to reassure him that he is still very special to you.

ADVANCE PREPARATION

It sometimes helps if you prepare the home child for his own feelings when the playgroup meets at his house. "When all the children come to playgroup at our house you'll probably feel funny to see them playing with your things at first." Then, when the time comes and the child does get mad, you can remind him that this is what you meant, and this makes it a little easier for him to accept.

REMOVING SOME TOYS

It also helps to allow the home child to decide which of his toys he really doesn't want to share, *for now*, and put them away on a high shelf before the others come. Then, if he gets upset when a child begins to play with one of his toys, you can tell him, "We put away all the special things you didn't want to share. Now, everything that's out is for all the children to play with." Some foxy children will propose that *everything* be put out of reach on playgroup mornings, but if this suggestion is treated with amusement rather than dismay, they will quickly see that this is impossible. You might remind them that they wouldn't like it if all the toys were put on high shelves at the other children's houses. Specific examples sometimes work to help a child be less possessive about his toys: "Do you remember that fire engine you liked so very much at Tom's house? You would miss playing with it if *he* decided to put it up on a shelf next time."

THE SPECIAL BLANKET

What about the special blanket, stuffed animal or cuddly object that so many playgroup-age children have in their rooms for security and comfort, and as an accessory for finger-sucking? Whereas the child might find strength in his own resources when faced with problems away from home and blanket, in his own playroom he might use his blanket as an easy out whenever any difficult situation comes up. This may keep him from really participating in playgroup activities when the group meets at his house. It is a good idea to put the blanket or object away for the playgroup morning, telling your child that the blanket is a special thing just for him at home, and it is better to put it away in a safe place when the other children come over to play. If he objects violently, you might compromise by having it somewhere in sight in the playroom, but out of reach. Then if he needs it, tell him you will get it down for him. Don't try to shame him out of it by telling him the other children will think he is a baby or anything of that sort. And if he really, *really* must have it, let him. After all, grownups have their accessory objects (cigarettes, pipes, chewing gum) that help them in social situations.

PART II

Activities

CHAPTER 7

Art

Meaning of art for young children

ART allows the young child to express himself at a time when he is still largely nonverbal.

In art activities the child has a great many choices which are only his: Which color shall I use? Where shall I place my figures? How large should they be? What should they look like? And so on. For someone who has little say about the things that happen to him, these can help build self-confidence.

The possibility of experimenting in art work is great and as the child does so, he also answers scientific questions that we take for granted: What happens to colors when they are mixed? How does paint change when it is mixed with water? What happens to clay when I squish it through my fingers?

Stages of development in art

When your child first begins drawing and painting, his work will look like meaningless scribbling. He scribbles because his movements in general are still very gross. The same sweeping movements which *may* get half the food from his clenched spoon into his mouth, get marks on the paper from a clenched crayon or a clenched brush. The marks are not planned. They hit the paper haphazardly, and the activity is its own reward.

As he gets more control, his markings become less random,

though they are still abstractions. To a large extent, it is still the process that counts. So if you ask your child what he is painting at this stage, you may get three completely different answers within five minutes.

Eventually a circle grows arms, a square gets windows, and the period of recognizable art begins. However, this art is still not *realistic,* so don't expect it to be in correct proportion and proper perspective. That won't happen for years. What your child-artist sees is colored by what he feels. If Suzy's best qualities are her cheerful disposition and her long hair, her friend Mary may paint Suzy with an extra-large head—featuring a smile and hair. On the other hand, if Mary and Suzy have had a fight, Mary may paint Suzy with an outsized scowl and an enormous hitting hand. This may be particularly true if Mary is still angry but hasn't been able to show it.

Guidelines for an art program

- Most important—*keep it free*. Let the children experiment as much as they want.
- *Be prepared for a mess*. To keep it down, put newspapers on the floor, make sure the playgroup youngsters put smocks on, and keep sponges and water nearby. This way it won't be overwhelming. If you are the kind of person who is really driven crazy by mess, provide activities other than painting and clay on your playgroup morning.
- Offer children as *many kinds of art materials* as possible.
- *Don't judge children's art by adult standards*. These very standards are the greatest block to their creativeness.
- *Give as few instructions as possible*. Too many instructions can limit experimentation.
- *Don't ask children, "What is that?"* The child may not have thought about a concrete object until you asked him. And thinking about a real object may get in the way of the feelings he was trying to express or the experimenting he was doing.
- *Show interest* in children's art and be generous with praise. Nothing encourages children more. But be sure you mean what

you say. Children will tend to distrust you if you have only lavish praise. Be specific in your praise. "I like your picture because the girl looks so cheerful." "I like the way the blue and the yellow meet in the middle."

However, don't comment at all on a child's art work itself, if he is not so much concerned with the end product as with mushing, sloshing and manipulating. It is better to make a general comment like, "You're really enjoying yourself today." Any remark which focuses on this child's work is focusing on something he wasn't concerned with, and is out of place.

• *Don't use coloring books.* By presenting a child with a book of adult drawings, you are saying, "This is the only way to draw." And your child's eventual reactions may be, "I can't draw."

• *Don't make models for children to copy,* even if they ask you to. If you do, you are again setting standards that are too high, as well as making it more difficult for a child to use his imagination.

If a child himself wants to make something "realistic" and asks for help, ask him helpful questions: Do you want to make a big dog or a little dog? What color do you want him to be? What kind of tail does he have? Does he have a sharp nose or a rounded nose? Often "Make me a dog," simply means that a child has not taken time to think through what he wants to make.

Another alternative is to provide a photograph (from a magazine, book or newspaper) for the child to look at.

If a child "can't draw a person," try giving him a mirror to look into.

Painting

EQUIPMENT

• An easel or some other place to paint
• Water paints, pre-mixed or powdered
• Paint containers
• Long-handled brushes of different sizes
• Paper. It can be newsprint, newspaper or any heavy paper
• Smocks, commercial or homemade

Easels

An easel is a good investment, and a good commercial two-sided easel which allows two children to paint at once will cost between $15 and $20. If there isn't enough floor space for it, a single easel which attaches to a wall or a door is available for around $10.

You may also make your own wall easel. Detailed instructions for making it can be found at the end of this chapter.

Paints

Water paints (poster paints or tempera) come both in liquid and powdered forms. If you get the prepared paints for your playgroup, you will find they are worth the difference in cost. Aside from being simpler to use because they are ready to pour and need no preparing, the liquid paints also have stronger colors. Bright colors are more appealing to children. Red, blue, yellow, black and white are the colors a child needs at first. From these he can learn to mix other colors himself, and later you can add other commercially prepared paints.

Don't buy the kind of water paints that come in sets of hard little cakes, and which we used to call watercolors when we were children. They are very frustrating for children this age. To get the colors they want takes much more control than most of them have. With poster paints, once the colors are mixed, you dip your brush, and you're in business. Watercolor brushes are also much smaller than most preschoolers can handle.

Paint Containers

For use at the easel, buy plastic jars with fitting caps made for the purpose, or save baby-food jars, 7-ounce peanut-butter jars, or even frozen juice cans and cover them with foil.

For table painting, use muffin tins. Use a different section for each color, one for water and one for mixing. The art classes at the Museum of Modern Art in New York City use glass furniture casters to hold paint. Keep them on a small, four-sided rust-proof tray, equipped with a water dish and a sponge or towel for wiping brushes.

Brushes

Buy good long-handled brushes with bristles in three different widths: ½", ¾", and 1". For two children to be able to paint simultaneously, it is best to have eight brushes. Of the eight, four should be 1", two should be ¾", and the other two should be ½". Each jar of paint should have its own brush. Brushes should be washed thoroughly in running warm water and left bristle-side up to dry.

Paper

Newsprint is the usual painting paper. Buy it in sheets at least 18" x 24". This is slightly wider than a single page of a conventional newspaper, and approximately as long. It can be bought reasonably from any newspaper printing shop where they discard the ends of newsprint rolls. For the youngest painters who are not yet interested in the end product, newspaper itself can be used.

Brown wrapping paper, either bought or saved from shirts, makes a nice variation.

Smocks

Every playgroup child should have his own smock. To make a simple smock, cut the sleeves off a man's shirt. It is then worn buttoned down the back.

An old shower sheet or plastic tablecloth can be converted into a smock. Cut a piece 48" long and 18" wide. Fold it in half, so that you now have a piece 24" long. Make a 6" slit along the center of the fold. If this isn't big enough for the child's head, the opening may be enlarged with an additional slit at right angles to the original one. If you want to be fancy, bind the edges with cloth tape. Make it tighter fitting by connecting the front to the back, and sewing a piece of elastic on each side at the waistline.

HOW TO BEGIN

Setting Up

When the playgroup arrives, the easel should be ready for painting. This means that paper is clamped on the easel with

Activities

DIAGRAM 7-1

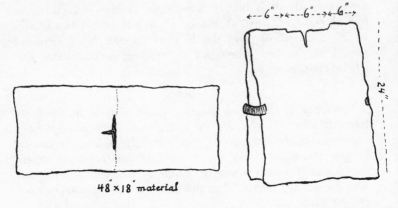

Laid Out for Cutting

$48'' \times 18'$ material

Completed

Paint Smock

DIAGRAM 7-2

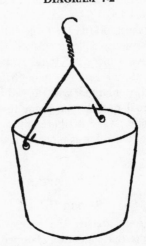

Brush Bucket

two large easel clips, or hung on two right-angle hooks which are screwed into the top corners of the easel.

Paints, bright and unmuddied, should be in the paint trough with a brush in each container. How many containers of paint to put out depends on whether the children have ever painted before. Start with two primary colors. If your group is composed of inexperienced three-year-olds, you may find that they paint with only one color anyway. Once they use both colors well, you can bring out the third. White and black can be added in the same way.

Don't forget to put out a container of water for rinsing brushes. It may be the one in diagram 7-2, or it may be a container like the ones holding paint.

Once the children have discovered that paints can be mixed, you will have to have jars handy for mixing.

If Encouragement Is Needed

Chances are that the prepared easel and the bright colors alone will attract the children. But if they don't, you can gently lead a child over to the easel. "Did you see the pretty red (blue, yellow) we have? See how it looks on the paper. I think you'll like it." If further encouragement is necessary, you can make an abstract mark or two on the paper, to give him an idea of what it will look like.

Setting Limits

When a child begins painting for the first time, it is a good idea to hold off on rules and regulations. Just let him get a good feeling about painting. When this step is passed and you feel it is time to set some limits, do so:

"This brush is for red. If you make a mistake, take a new brush or rinse your brush in the water."

"Did you mean to make orange in that jar? Next time you want to make orange, ask me for another jar to make it in and you'll have orange and red both."

"Wipe your brush on the edge of the can this way before you use it." (Wait for a few strokes.) "You see, you don't have to make drippy lines unless you want to."

The Finished Product

Children usually like to have their names on their work—but not always. So before you automatically write a child's name on his painting (or anything else he has done), ask him whether you should. If he says yes, ask him where he wants it printed.

Once the paintings are finished, they can be draped over the shower-curtain rod to dry. They can also be clothespinned to a string stretched across a room. If you have an old indoor drying rack, it will serve. Newsprint has a tendency to crack after it has been painted. If that matters to you, dry the paintings more slowly by spreading them on several thicknesses of dampened newspaper.

CLEAN-UP TIPS

• When you are ready to put the paints away, wipe the lips of all jars with a tissue. A touch of petroleum jelly around the lip will make it easier to open next time.

• Paint troughs tend to get caked with paint. This makes it more difficult to fit the paint containers into them. If your trough is an open rectangle, line it with a cardboard milk container, one long side cut out. If your trough is a board with circles cut out for individual containers, cover it entirely with a long piece of aluminum foil. Place your paint containers where the circles should be, and push down. These liners can be discarded and replaced often.

• You can provide water for cleaning brushes in a container made from a plastic bleach bottle and a clothes hanger. It can be hung on the easel support. When the painting session is over, drop the brushes in and carry them to the sink without dripping paint all over.

Fingerpainting

As the name implies, fingerpainting involves making pictures not with brushes, but with fingers, and it is a rare preschooler who doesn't like to fingerpaint. Having just gone through the experience of toilet training, he finds it quite a switch to be invited suddenly to make a mess. But he is quite willing to take advantage of the opportunity. The child who doesn't want to fingerpaint is usually the one who needs it most. So try to encourage all the children to participate without making an issue of it. Once the hesitant child finally gives it a try, he usually finds that he likes it and works eagerly for a long time.

Fingerpainting is also known to have a calming effect on children. It is a good activity to initiate when a child is wound up and having a wild morning.

EQUIPMENT

- Fingerpaints, commercial or homemade.
- Fingerpaint paper, shiny shelf paper or a washable tray or tabletop.

Paint

You can buy fingerpaints or make them. The children will enjoy helping you.

Recipe for homemade fingerpaints

Beat together ½ cup of *instant* cold-water starch,
  ½ cup of soap *flakes* (not powder or detergent), and
  ⅝ cup (5 oz.) of water.
Beat them until they are the consistency of whipped potatoes. Add food coloring to give them a vibrant color.

Fingerpaint Paper and Substitutes

Most three-year-olds and even some four-year-olds don't care whether they take their finished paintings home or not. If this is the case, let them paint right on a table that has a formica, porcelain or plastic top. You can also tape or tack a piece of oilcloth to a table top, or give each child a plastic tray or aluminum cookie sheet and allow him to paint on the bottom of it.

If the children in the playgroup care about the finished product, supply them with fingerpaint paper. Shiny shelving paper is almost as good. Or place a piece of newsprint on the painting which was made on a table or a tray. Run the flat of your hand gently across the paper from one side to the other, until all the paper has been handled. When you pick up the newsprint, it will have a copy of the painting on it.

HOW TO BEGIN

The table, tray or paper to be used for fingerpainting must first be moistened with a damp sponge. You may have to do this for the children because the surface needs to be wet without being soaked. Put about a spoonful of paint on the surface with a plastic spoon or a tongue depressor. Let the child coat the area with his open palm until the paint is used up. Give him more—a spoonful at a time—until the entire surface is coated. He then makes his picture by rubbing his fingers (or hands or arms) in the paint, leaving a design in it. If he doesn't like what he has done, he can "erase" it by recoating the surface.

The tables and trays are easily washed up with sponges and water, and the fingerpainters usually join in, this being part of the fun.

Gadget painting

There are other kinds of painting besides brush painting and fingerpainting. These are described below. The children will enjoy them, and they will add variety to your art program.

When you introduce a new kind of painting, have all the materials ready when the children come in. You will probably have to sit at the table with them for the first time, giving specific instructions, step by step, without actually doing it yourself, until they have mastered the technique. Then you can probably let them do it alone.

SPONGE PAINTING

For sponge painting, cut a dish sponge into 1"–2" pieces. A standard 4½" x 3" sponge will give you about six paint sponges. Pour somewhat thick poster paints into the cups of a muffin tin, and place a pile of paper towels next to the tin, to blot the sponges. Sponge painting can be done on newsprint, construction paper or any other kind of paper. Children enjoy making their own wrapping paper by sponge painting on tissue paper.

The procedure is simple. Each color has its own sponge. The child takes the sponge, dips it gently into the right color, blots it on the paper towel, and finally pats it on the paper. The more gently this is done, the more you can see of the design left by the sponge cells. But let the children discover this for themselves. If they want to smear with the sponges, let them.

STRAW PAINTING

Children usually love straw painting. They will need some watered poster paints, a drinking straw apiece, and paper of any kind to paint on.

Pour about a tablespoon of paint in the middle of each child's paper. He can then direct it all over the paper by blowing a stream of air at it through the straw. The straw should be held about an inch above the paper. It should not touch the paint. If the children insist on trying to drink the paint, forget about this kind of painting.

PIPE CLEANER, TOOTHPICK, OR SWAB PAINTING

Children get so accustomed to broad brushstrokes, that the smallness of the lines produced becomes the attraction of pipe cleaner, toothpick or swab painting.

Fill a muffin tin with paints as for sponge painting. The children paint by using cotton swabs or pipe cleaners instead of brushes. It is a good idea to get white pipe cleaners, because the children get sidetracked into playing with the attractive colored ones.

STRING PAINTING

The effects you get with string painting depend on the kind of string or yarn you use and the thickness of your paint. The best combination is a matter of personal choice.

Pour paint into a pie tin, soup plate or other wide-mouthed dish. Fold any 8½″ x 11″ paper into two 5½″ halves, and lay it open in front of the child. He then coats all of a piece of string in the paint except for the end he is holding. When the string is coated, he lays it on the right-hand half of his paper, closing the left half over it. Using one hand to hold the paper closed, he pulls the string out through the bottom with the other hand.

If you prefer, he can lay the string on an unfolded piece of paper, and use another piece for the top piece.

He can make multicolored paintings by using several different paints and strings on the same sheet of paper.

This activity is fun, but may be too hard for three-year-olds since it involves a great deal of coordination.

DIAGRAM 7-3

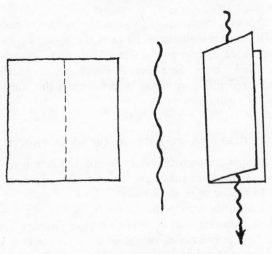

String Painting

CARDBOARD-ROLL PRINTING

The simplest kind of printing can be done with the cardboard roll found inside toilet paper, paper towels, aluminum foil and some plastic wrappings. Don't use the shiny rolls used for other plastic wrappings because they are not absorbent enough.

To make a roll print, start with muffin tins filled with paint, as for sponge painting. The child dips one end of the roll in the paint and imprints circles on his paper. He can turn the roll over and use the other end for another color. The longer rolls can be cut in half with a sharp knife to make two rolls.

VEGETABLE PRINTING

Potato printing is an old-time favorite of all children. But any similar vegetable—carrot, turnip, horseradish—will do as well. You can use a good cork, but this may be harder to carve. You will have to do the carving since this involves cutting with a sharp knife.

Cut the vegetable to give you a flat surface. Leave the child enough to hold comfortably. Draw a simple design on it—a star, a circle, a square, a moon, a triangle. You can either hollow out the design, or cut down the vegetable around it, leaving the design raised. Now the child can take over. After blotting the vegetable on a paper towel, he paints the raised part with a brush and poster paints. Finally he can print the design on the paper. If you use textile (batik) paints, the design can be printed on fabric and the children can make mats or other gifts.

DIAGRAM 7-4

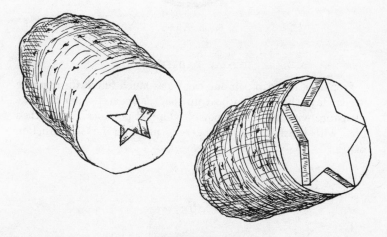

Vegetable Printers

SPOOL PRINTING

To make a spool printer, make a design with a pipe cleaner and glue it to the end of an empty thread spool. Another way is to cut a design out of the thin sheets of sponge which are sold for dishwashing, and to glue that to the end of the spool. Holding the spool as a handle, the child dips the design into some paint, blots it, and stamps his design onto his paper.

DIAGRAM 7-5

Spool Printer

SOAP PAINTING

Preparing for soap painting can be as much fun as the painting itself. Have the children beat up soap *flakes* and water to make a mixture with the consistency of whipped potatoes. This is then used with brushes or even fingers to paint on dark construction paper.

Collage

Collages are abstract constructions made by pasting rather than by painting. Children enjoy it because it has a messy element to it in the paste, while essentially being a neat medium, offering them lots of opportunity for choice and organization.

EQUIPMENT

- Collage materials for pasting
- Scissors that really cut
- Paste. It may be commercial or homemade, solid or liquid
- Background paper

Collage Materials

Anything that can be pasted makes good material. A list of suggested materials follows this section. Once your playgroup has begun to make collages, you will find yourself looking at everything with new eyes, and things that you once would have thrown away unthinkingly, you will now add to your collage hoard. Keep a special box for this collection.

When you prepare materials, it is always better to cut them into abstract shapes than into recognizable outlines. If you are using gift paper or wall paper that has pictures rather than an overall pattern, cut it into such pieces that the pictures are not recognizable. Giving children realistic cuttings is suggesting themes for their pictures and limiting their own imaginations. Make your pieces at least ½″ x ½″, or they will be too small for the children to handle easily. To vary your pieces, you can cut them with pinking shears occasionally, or tear them. Even children who cannot use scissors can tear and enjoy preparing for collage this way. Once they have learned to cut, leave some large pieces in the tray, so they can have the opportunity to cut their own shapes if they want to.

The best kind of collage tray has divisions—one for each kind of scrap. It may be an old cutlery tray or a sectionalized dish, or you can use a separate box for each kind of material.

Here are some of the endless possibilities of collage materials:

Fabrics of all textures:
  smooth (polished cotton)
  raised (corduroy)
  rough (tweed)
  soft (velvet)
  scratchy (burlap)
  Save both solid and patterned fabrics.
Papers:
  paper doilies

construction paper
gift paper
newspaper
origami paper
cellophane
greeting cards
small boxes
candy and cupcake cups
candy boxes and candy
    wrappers
excelsior
cardboard dividers from be-
    tween layers of fruit or
    eggs
aluminum foil
straws
wallpaper
photographic paper
caps from glass milkbottles
corrugated cardboard
Easter basket "grass"
Miscellaneous:
    fur
    feathers
    absorbent cotton
    rug scraps
    linoleum scraps
    oilcloth
    rug underlay

sequins
sequin ribbon
small buttons
cork
toothpicks
glitter
yarn
string
uncooked macaroni products
uncooked dried peas and beans
dry cereal
small shells
gravel and sand
leather
wood shavings
theatrical gelatines
egg shells: Shells from hard-
boiled eggs are the easiest
to use. If you use other
shells, be careful to re-
move all the egg and egg
membrane before you dye
the shells with vegetable
coloring or they will ab-
sorb most of the dye.
Crush the shells with a
rolling pin or pass them
through a food mill.

Scissors

Cutting is very hard for little children, but it is something they all want to learn. Few things please them more than mastery of this activity. Don't make it harder for them by buying cheap scissors that don't cut properly and that bend easily. Sturdy, blunt-nosed scissors that do a good job cost at least 50¢. If any of the children are lefthanded, try to find them the special lefthanded scissors that are available.

Paste

The most widely used paste is the solid, white kind commonly referred to as *library paste*. Buy an individual container for each child: these have brushes or plastic spreaders. Once the containers are empty, you can refill them from a larger jar. Library paste does not spill when the jar is dropped or tipped. On the other hand, it is harder for the children to use in small quantities and their collages often have lumps of excess paste under the pasted pieces.

Liquid paste does not have this disadvantage. Since it is fluid, its applicator brush can be wiped on the edge of the paste pot. This allows more control and encourages neatness. It has the decided disadvantage of being spillable. One word of warning: liquid paste is *not* the same as glue, so read labels carefully.

You can make *old-fashioned paste* by mixing flour and water, until you get the consistency you want. It is not as satisfactory as the commercial variety, but children enjoy making it. Give each child his own paste in a jar top or plastic coffee-can top, and have him use his fingers or a tongue depressor as a spreader. Or put some of it in a squeeze bottle such as baby lotions or liquid detergents come in, and have him squeeze out the amount he wants to use.

Background Paper

Any kind of paper which is at least as heavy as construction paper may be used as a background for collage. It may be large or small, white or colored. Brown wrapping paper, shirt cardboards and even boxes, paper plates and cans may be used.

HOW TO BEGIN

The day you introduce collage-making, prepare the worktable with a pair of scissors and a paste pot at each child's place. In the middle of the table, put the tray containing only one kind of collage material. Pieces of colored construction paper cut into simple abstract shapes are a good first choice. Next to the tray lay a stack of background papers. Explain to the children that they can make pictures by pasting pieces from the tray onto the paper. This is not the time to tell them how to paste neatly.

First collages are often nothing more than one or two scraps on an entire sheet of paper. Others consist of a series of scraps pasted one on top of the other like a pile of flapjacks.

Once the children are happy making collages, you can show them that liquid paste needs to be wiped on the lip of the pot, that smaller amounts of solid paste make for less lumpiness, and that the background paper won't be so sticky if they spread the paste on the shape itself ("like buttering bread") rather than on the paper. Many of them will have discovered this for themselves.

Vary your tray often, or the children may become bored. Add more cuttings to your collage tray.

Once you have introduced the children to collage-making, devote one section of the art shelf to it. Leave a full tray, paste and scissors, and background paper there. When the children feel like making collages, they can take the things to the table, and set to work.

COLLAGE IDEAS

• A single-color tray—for example, all cuttings some shade of blue, but of different textures: shiny paper, construction paper, corduroy, velvet, wallpaper, yarn, and so on.

• A tray of one texture (smooth, for example), but of many different colors and patterns. Refer to the patterns by their names. You will be surprised how quickly children learn what plaid, striped, checked and flowered mean when they learn it in this context.

• A session during which the children paste up things they have gathered outdoors: fall leaves, acorn caps, small twigs, seed pods, "polynoses." This kind of collage is especially exciting.

• Collage and any kind of painting combined. The child can superimpose the collage on the paper that has a painting on it, or he can make a collage first and add touches of paint later.

Clay and other modeling materials

THE MEANING OF MODELING TO YOUNG CHILDREN

For most children, modeling is the first three-dimensional art form. Like fingerpainting, modeling allows them direct contact with materials, and invites them to mess. Modeling materials are especially soothing to a child who needs to let off steam. Forbidden to throw things or to hit other children, he can be encouraged to let go by hitting and pounding clay. Hitting clay is much less frightening to an angry child than is any other form of destructiveness, because he can't really destroy it, and he can actually rebuild it to its original form.

STAGES OF DEVELOPMENT IN MODELING

Young children push, pull, squeeze, pat and feel modeling materials, having a wonderful time before it ever occurs to them to "make something"—however abstract.

This stage is followed by a period during which balls, snakes and pancakes are mass produced. These shapes eventually give way to more complicated ones, made by adding pieces of clay to each other, or by pulling details out of one large mass of clay. Which technique a child uses depends on how he sees things, and neither is preferable. Finally the recognizable stage is reached, as it was in painting.

KINDS OF CLAY

There is no substitute for the water-base, self-hardening gray type sold as *moist clay*. It is not the same as the brightly colored nonhardening *modeling clay* available at the five-and-ten, which is either plastic or oil-based clay. Modeling clay tends to be too hard for little children to work unless it is first kneaded by an adult, while moist clay can be softened easily by working, and its consistency can be changed by the addition of water. If the child wishes to make a permanent object, he can't with modeling clay because it won't harden, whereas moist clay dries thoroughly in several days. Once it is hard, it can be painted.

Moist clay is sold ready for use in 5, 25, and 50-lb. packages. The cost is reasonable and a 25-lb. package of clay lasts a long time. Clay also comes as clay flour which must be mixed with water at home, but this is really a great deal of trouble and not worth the saving.

STORING CLAY

Since clay does harden, it is sold in plastic bags. As plastic rips easily, transfer the clay, bag and all, to a container with a tight-fitting cover, such as a plastic garbage can with a clip-on lid. A wet cloth laid across the top of the clay keeps it from drying out.

It is not necessary to dig out the clay with your fingernails. Pull down the bottom bar of a wire clothes hanger and use that to slice it as you would use a cheese cutter to slice cheese.

If the clay gets dry, either make the topcloth sopping wet before putting it away, or knead water into each piece of clay before giving it to a child. If you want to salvage pieces that have dried out completely, break them into tiny pieces with a hammer, and put them into another plastic bag with a lot of water. Stir and knead this mixture periodically for several days, until you again have moist clay. Lots of newspaper makes a good blotter if you have added too much water at any time.

PLAYDOUGH

If moist clay is unavailable, playdough makes a more satisfactory substitute than does modeling clay. It is more easily workable, but tends to crumble when dry.

Besides being a substitute for clay, playdough is an excellent "food" when the children play house.

Commercial playdough is available, but the children enjoy making their own. Homemade playdough is just as good as the commercial kind, and since vegetable coloring can be blended, more varieties of dough can be made at home than can be bought.

Playdough Recipe

Stir together 2 cups of unsifted flour and
        1 cup of salt, with
        1 cup (approximately) of water containing food coloring, and
        2 tablespoons of cooking oil.
Knead the ingredients together until you get the consistency of bread dough.

WORK SPACE

If the children's worktable is washable, clay can be worked right on it. Otherwise tack or tape a piece of oilcloth to it, *shiny side down,* and use that for your modeling surface. Don't use newspaper to protect the table. It will dry out the clay.

If the children are using playdough and your worktable needs protection, let them use it on the shiny side of a piece of oilcloth which has been well secured to the table.

HOW TO BEGIN

If Encouragement Is Needed

The morning you introduce clay or playdough, have a 3"–4" ball of it at each child's place. Probably you will not have to do anything else, but if nothing happens, sit down with the children at the table and start working a piece of clay yourself. Pat, squeeze, roll, but don't make anything specific. This is often encouragement enough to get the children started. "How does it feel?" "What a flat piece!" "I wonder what will happen if I squeeze (pat, push, poke) this piece?"—these are examples of the innocuous questions that lead to further experimentation. These kinds of questions and this approach are also helpful if children get bogged down once they have started using clay.

Because claywork is three-dimensional, even abstractions seem to suggest something real more often than painted abstractions do. Don't let this fool you into admiring a "snake" or a "cake" or a "snowman." Admire the length, the smoothness, the round-ness of an object, but don't focus on its realness, unless the child has volunteered that he has a specific object in mind.

Accessories

Once you feel the children have really tried out the clay but have begun to get a little bored with it, bring out the accessories: rolling pins, dried beans, macaroni, toothpicks, buttons and pipe cleaners. It should take many sessions before they need them—if at all. If you bring out the accessories too early, the children may get into the rut of being unable to work without them. You will find that a modeling session then becomes the occasion for the production of endless numbers of birthday cakes.

When playdough is used as "food," you can supply the children with small rolling pins, cookie cutters, cookie and garlic presses, and icing tubes to use with it. Give them a small dish of flour, or a spice jar that has a large-holed shaker top, or a powdered-sugar shaker with flour in it.

When a child is finished playing with clay and he does not want to keep his work, he should roll it back into a ball and return it to the container.

At the end of the session, provide a basin of water and give each child a sponge so that he can help clean the table. Occasionally he may need a brush or metal scourer if some clay is stuck.

Crayons

Crayons offer many more possibilities than most people realize, but crayoning is still less satisfying than are the messier art forms. Crayons are fine, but they should not be used as a substitute for the other art media.

KINDS OF CRAYONS

It's best to buy thick crayons which are easier to hold and to use for children whose muscle control is still developing. If the children seem to hold them awkwardly because they are too long, or even if they are being too "careful not to break them," they are not getting full use out of the crayons, and you will need to break them in half.

If you have a choice, buy hexagonal crayons, or crayons with one flat side. They don't roll and the prepared flat side makes large-surface crayoning easier.

USING CRAYONS

Crayons have three usable surfaces—not just the point. The point makes a fine line, but the flat end opposite the point makes a wide one. The side of a crayon can cover a large surface with shaded lines rather than the dark solid lines made by the ends. Peel crayons before you give them to the children, and they will discover these possibilities more easily.

Children can blend colors to get new ones, but this will work well only with good-quality crayons. Children's crayons contain wax, and the amount of wax used and the way it is mixed with the other ingredients determine whether a crayon is a good one. The wax rubs off a bad crayon too easily, so it rubs off the paper, too. Stay away from crayons that have a waxy look. If you're not sure, make a mark and scratch it with your fingernail. Only a small amount of wax should come off, and the color on the paper should remain dark.

DIAGRAM 7-6

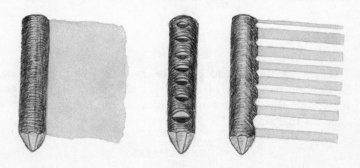

Notch the sides of some crayons. The effect is quite different from that attained by using the smooth, flat side of the stick.

CRAYON ACTIVITIES

Textured Crayoning

An irregular and interesting effect is achieved by putting a piece of corrugated cardboard, wire mesh, sandpaper, or stiff netting under the paper to be crayoned.

Wax Resist

Since crayons contain wax, they repel any water-base paints that are brushed over them. The children first crayon their papers. Then they brush poster paints on the entire surface. The paints are absorbed by those portions of the paper that are free of wax.

At Easter time, hard-cooked eggs can be decorated with crayons before they are dyed. The same principle is involved.

Textile Crayoning

Although crayoning is usually done on paper, the children will enjoy making their designs on a piece of fabric. Unbleached muslin or old linen sheets provide this cheaply, but any kind of smooth, tightly woven fabric will do.

To set the design, iron it with a warm iron, using a damp press cloth.

Chalk

Chalk has its classical place at the blackboard, but it can be used on paper as well. Any paper which is not smooth and shiny, and which is at least as heavy as construction paper, is good for this purpose.

USING CHALKS

Chalk comes in two varieties: hard and soft. Get soft chalk in the thickest available sticks. It rubs off readily, so children can make marks without pushing too hard. A broad spectrum of vivid colors is available, and new colors can be blended by rubbing one color on top of another. Like crayons, chalk has the two ends and the side of the stick available for different effects. It also comes in square or hexagonal sticks, as well as the round.

Although soft chalk makes a good medium for three- and four-year-olds because of its softness, it also creates paintings that smear very easily. To minimize the smearing, you will have to use a fixative.

Commercial fixatives are available, but it is not necessary to use them. Diluted *whole* milk (about 1:1 with water) or diluted buttermilk does a satisfactory job. The finished painting can be dipped in a shallow pan of fixative or sprayed with the milk fixative. Corrugated cardboard, wire mesh, sandpaper and stiff net can be placed under the paper before chalking to get textured effects.

Constructions: mobiles and stabiles

Mobiles and stabiles can be thought of as three-dimensional collages. The same kinds of things that made good collage materials, make good construction materials. In this case, they are attached to each other by pieces of wire or thread rather than by paste. The mobile is free-hanging so that currents of air can move it, while the stabile is fixed.

Stabiles can be simple enough for the youngest playgroupers to make. Mobiles are more difficult and often present too many problems for three-year-olds.

EQUIPMENT

- wire of different gauges
- wire cutters
- stabile bases, such as clay, styrofoam or pieces of soft wood
- mobile supports such as pipe cleaners, wire hangers or dowels
- assorted materials for constructions

Wire

Wire is used in most constructions. It can be curved, bent or curled. It can be twisted to stay in place. It is sharp enough to be pushed through paper and many fabrics and cardboards. It is stiff enough so that beads, buttons and macaroni can be strung on it easily.

Get various gauges of copper and brass wire, heavy enough to withstand bending, but not so heavy that the children have difficulty bending it. (Gauges between 16 and 24 are about right.)

84 · *Activities*

It is available in spools and rolls at the five-and-ten and at hardware stores, or in pre-cut lengths which are sold as florist's wire in florist-supply and hobby shops. Pipe cleaners and bell wire come in several colors.

In addition to these, you will need a spool of fine wire. Since it can be twisted in place, it will be used to attach materials to the supporting wires (or to any support), because few preschoolers can tie a knot. If any of them can, you can substitute coat and rug thread or string for the fine wire.

Wire Cutters

You will need to cut the heavier wire for the children with wire cutters. They can cut the very fine wire with their regular scissors.

Stabile Bases

Clay is the easiest stabile base. The children stick wire, straws of various lengths, pipe cleaners, feathers or other things into a mass of moist clay, which is then allowed to dry.

Styrofoam, the lightweight plastic used to make Christmas ornaments, is available in the florist department of the dime store throughout the year. Wire and toothpicks go into it very easily.

Pieces of pine or soft composition board such as homosote make good bases. The child lays a piece of support wire across it, and hammers a ⅜" wood staple to hold the wire in place. He then bends the wire upward at any angle. You may have to prepare this kind of base for the younger playgroupers. More than one piece of wire can be used on the same board to make a more complicated stabile.

Mobile Supports

A simple mobile is made by attaching things to a free-swinging pipe cleaner or a length of ¼" dowel. Extra-long pipe cleaners can be bought from florists or hobby shops.

The children can follow that mobile with a slightly more advanced one, which they make by looping one piece of pipe cleaner (or bell wire) around another, forming an X.

DIAGRAM 7-7

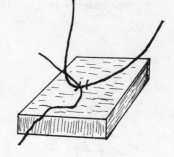

Simple   **More Complex**

Wooden Stabile Bases

DIAGRAM 7-8

Pipe Cleaner Mobile Support

A wire clothes hanger makes another simple mobile support. The children hang things from any part of it with fine wire or string. A series of hangers can be hooked to each other to make a more complex mobile. The hanger can be twisted for variety.

DIAGRAM 7-9

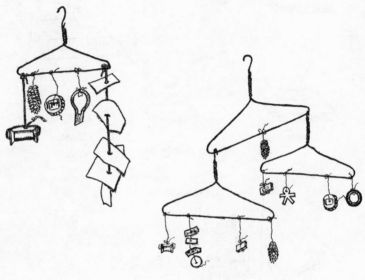

Simple   More. Complex

Wire Hanger Mobile Supports

Sequin ribbon and cardboard with holes punched in it make good mobile supports, as do stiff netting such as buckram or petitpoint backing. Wire or thin dowels can be threaded through the holes to form the arms from which things will be hung. This can be done in several tiers as children get more adept.

The children can build a mobile using Tinker Toys. The dowels, stuck into the round pieces, serve as arms from which to hang things.

DIAGRAM 7-10

Punched Cardboard Mobile Support

Stabile-Mobile

One variety of construction is a cross between a stabile and a mobile. The children first attach support wires or dowels to a stabile base. Then, rather than stringing things along the supports, they connect the things to the ends of the supports with a length of fine wire or string.

Since the base of a stabile-mobile is stationary, only parts of the construction move, making this a good preface to free-swinging mobiles.

Coiling one of the support wires by twining it around a pencil converts it into a spring, which has movement of its own, whether anything is hung from it or not.

MATERIALS FOR CONSTRUCTIONS; SOME SUGGESTIONS

Anything which can give height makes good stabile material. In addition to wires, you can use:

straws	dowels
feathers	swabs
round toothpicks (colored and plain)	ice-cream sticks

Anything which comes with a hole is a natural for being strung on a construction:

buttons	certain dry cereals
beads	washers
sequins	woodworking nuts
sequin ribbon	cut straws
macaroni products	

Most papers, cardboards and fabrics can be pierced by wire or can be punched with a paperpunch to make a hole for stringing.

Other things hang from mobiles when the end of a fine wire is wrapped around them and twisted to hold:

toothpicks (colored and plain)	tongue depressors
corks	ice-cream sticks, and
dowels	bolts, to name a few.
swabs	

DIAGRAM 7-11

Stabile-Mobile

HOW TO BEGIN
Stabiles

Stabiles are generally simpler constructions than mobiles, so it is a good idea to begin with them.

The first stabile should be an easy one. Use a clay or styrofoam base, toothpicks and multicolored construction paper cut into abstract shapes for a good beginning. Have a piece of clay or styrofoam at each child's place when he comes in. Put your collage tray containing the paper and the toothpicks in the middle of the table. Explain to the children that they are going to make a new kind of design. Tell them they can stick the toothpicks into the styrofoam (clay) anywhere they want to. Then they can add to their design by attaching papers to the toothpicks. It doesn't take too much of a push to get the tip of the toothpick through the paper.

DIAGRAM 7-12

Simple Clay Base Stabile

For the next stabile, substitute wire or pipe cleaners for the toothpicks. Use paper again, although it can be a different assortment than the first time.

After that, you can put out wire and toothpicks and more varied materials, and give the children a larger choice.

Mobiles

A piece of strong cord strung across the width of the play-room or across a very wide doorway is the best arrangement for mobile work. If this is not possible, tie the cord between two chairs that have been weighted to prevent them from moving. Tie a string to the cord for each child. It should be long enough so that its free end will be at a convenient working height. If you decide that the first mobiles will be made with a wire hanger base, tie a hanger to each of the pieces of string. Since the children will have had experience with stabiles, the collage tray can be sitting on the worktable full of a variety of materials.

Tell the children they are going to make designs similar to stabiles, but that these will move. (If the mobiles move too much, you may have to help by holding them still.)

A Group Mobile

The most practical mobile to try with three-year-olds is a group mobile. Each child can make some contribution and feel a sense of accomplishment when it is finished, while it is a rare three-year-old who could make a mobile alone. With only one mobile to work on, you can help the children better than if you had to divide your attention among several projects. Besides having this practical value, group mobilemaking, like all group activities, has its social and fun value, so don't overlook it for four-year-olds as well.

Puppets

Puppets have an important part in children's dramatic play. This aspect of puppets, and directions for adult-made puppets, are dealt with in Chapter 15. This chapter discusses a few simple puppets that preschoolers can make themselves.

PAPER BAG PUPPETS

Give each child a brown paper lunch bag, and have him fill it out with wads of newspaper. You may have to crumple the paper first. When the bag is full, the child inserts a toilet-paper roll into the opening, while you close the bag around it with string or wire. The roll serves jointly as a neck for the puppet and a handle for the puppeteer. The child then paints or glues features on the puppet, or uses a combination of the two techniques.

Stick Puppets

Once a child has begun to draw recognizable figures, he can make a very simple puppet by cutting out a figure he has drawn, and gluing or stapling it onto a tongue depressor.

Children can make another kind of stick puppet by pasting geometric shapes onto a tongue depressor to form human figures. The shapes can be bought prepackaged, or you can cut them yourself.

Developing concepts through art

As children work with the various art media, they begin to observe and to learn their properties. With your help they can learn the names that go with these qualities.

DIAGRAM 7-13

Paper Bag Puppet

Activities

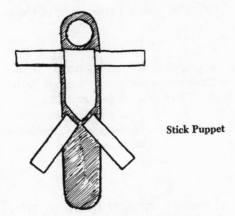

Stick Puppet

DIAGRAM 7-14

PAINTING

- Paints can be mixed to make new colors. Red and yellow make orange; red and blue make purple; blue and yellow make green; red, blue and yellow make brown. White lightens any other color.
- Adding water to paint makes it thinner. If it is very thick, adding water makes it more usable. Too much water makes paint so thin, it doesn't hide the paper.
- Paint drips. The thinner it is, the more it drips.
- When paint is wet, it looks shiny. It is duller when it is dry.
- Paint is darker when it is wet and lightens as it dries.

COLLAGE

- All kinds of textures are used as collage materials, and they feel and look very different from each other. A few are rough, smooth, shiny, dull, scratchy; striped, plaid, solid, checked, dotted.
- Paste dries if it is left uncovered. The outside dries first. Sometimes you can use the paste underneath the crust.
- Paste is usually smooth, even if it is sticky.

MOBILES-STABILES

- Different-sized things have to be placed carefully to make things balance. Sometimes you can balance a construction by moving the hangings to another spot on the wire. Sometimes it takes a lot of things to balance one heavy piece.

• The thicker a piece of wire is, the stronger it is.

CRAYONS AND CHALK

• Crayons and chalk rub off the stick to make their marks. That's why they get shorter as you use them, and sometimes rub off on your clothes.

Making a wall easel

RIGID WALL EASEL

To make your own wall easel, start with a sheet of plywood 20" x 26". Attach a 2½" wide wood lath across the back of the plywood at the bottom. This will hold the easel out from the wall. Use angle irons to give extra support.

DIAGRAM 7-15

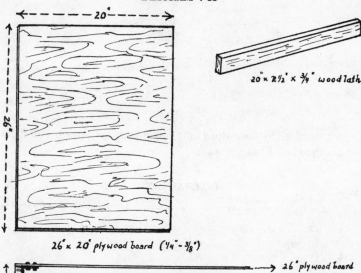

20" x 2½" x ¾" wood lath

26" x 20" plywood board (¼" - ⅜")

26" plywood board

← Angle iron
← wood lath

ACTIVITIES FOR THE FIRST DAY

Attach a wooden cheesebox to the bottom front to serve as a paint tray. Attach the top of the easel to the wall with long nails or screws.

DIAGRAM 7-16

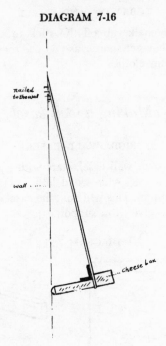

A pair of rigid door stops or a towel rack can also be used to angle the easel from the wall.

DIAGRAM 7-17

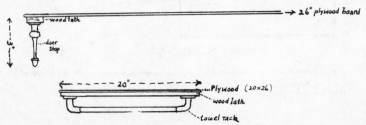

COLLAPSIBLE WALL EASEL

To make a wall easel that can collapse flush against the wall, attach a pair of laths to each other with a pair of hinges. Attach one to the top of the plywood sheet, and the other to the wall.

The wood attached to the bottom of the plywood needs to be about 6″ wide. Attach it with hinges rather than with angle irons.

DIAGRAM 7-18

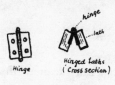

Hinge

Hinged laths
(Cross section)

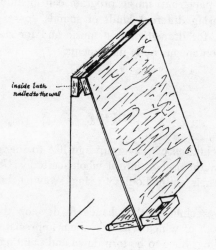

inside lath
nailed to the wall

Cheese box
paintholder

CHAPTER 8

Music

Music for young children can be more than just listening and singing. Your playgroup music program can include the opportunity for hearing different kinds of sounds, for experimenting with rhythms, for dramatizing to music and for responding to music with spontaneous body movements.

Singing

Almost all children of playgroup age like to sing. When they do, they throw themselves into it wholeheartedly. Unlike adults, children use their entire bodies to sing, swaying, bouncing and jiggling.

Singing gives children the chance to develop their ear and their pitch, both of which will help them appreciate music.

Block buildings have to be torn down and paintings eventually dry or tear, but a child will carry the song he has learned with him, as tangible proof of his success.

Folk songs and nursery rhymes that the young child learns have merit as both music and language. As he grows older and learns history and related subjects, these songs and rhymes will gain even more meaning.

Like any other group activity, singing is fun because it gives children the opportunity to do things together.

WHAT TO SING

There are many kinds of songs you can sing with children. A few contemporary songs written for children are good, but for the most part, folk songs and Mother Goose rhymes are more dependable. The qualities that make folk songs last through the years also make them meaningful and enjoyable to the children.

At the end of this chapter you will find a numbered list of useful song collections and recordings especially good for young children. In general, choose songs that

- Have simple words and music.
- Appeal directly to the child by using his name, some article of his clothing, or something he has done.
- Have repeated phrases or very simple rhymes, so that they can be learned quickly and easily. The satisfaction of learning a few songs with ease will encourage children to learn more of them, so that after a while you can introduce more complicated songs.
- Include some action, such as "She'll Be Coming Round the Mountain" (#9) and "Shoo, Fly" (#6).
- Have silly-sounding phrases like "Duck went slishy-sloshy," ("Bought Me a Cat," #9), or "To my wing wong waddle, to my jack straw saddle" ("Swapping Song," #6). As difficult as these nonsense syllables seem, the children work hard at them because they like them, and often learn silly syllables they like more quickly than simple phrases that don't appeal to them.
- Are about subjects that interest young children, such as other children, animals, transportation, the seasons, cowboys, approaching holidays, to name a few.
- Have something to do with their lives at the moment. For example, a rain song on a rainy day, or a song about farm animals before or after a trip to a farm.

INTRODUCING SONGS

A good song for your first singing session is one that uses all the children's names. Choose a very simple one like "Mary Wore a Red Dress" (#6) and sing it, substituting each child's name and something he is wearing. Encourage the children to sing along with you. Some other suitable songs that can be used this way are "Walk Along, John," (#9), "I Wonder What Tina Can Do?" (#36) and "Jenny Jenkins" (#6).

Don't worry about how well you can sing. Children respond to your enthusiasm rather than to your voice quality. What's more, you'll find that the more you sing, the better and freer your singing will become.

After a few sessions you might try a simple song with few words like "Muffin Man" (#2) or "Pick a Bale of Cotton" (#20). Giving the children an idea of what the song is about before you sing it, or some special effect to listen for, makes any song you wish to sing with them more appealing. It will interest the children to know that once the muffin man came around like the ice-cream man does today, and that cotton is a plant that has to be picked. Having told them that, sing the song through in a simple voice. Sing it again slowly and invite the children to sing along with you.

You will find that children pick up most songs quickly. If a song is still badly garbled after two sessions, it is too hard or not meaningful enough. Drop it.

IMPROVISING WITH SONGS

Many songs can be changed by you or by the children to suit the needs of the moment. These new songs can be particularly useful at difficult transition times.

Four playgroup children dragging home from the park can be speeded along with the "Step Song" (#13), substituting the children's names for "Jeffie." "Walk along, John, with your paper collar on," (#9) becomes "Walk along, Sallie, just a few steps more." They can also puff home as a train to "Train is A-coming" (#9) with each child playing a specific role.

> "Mikey is the engine, oh yes.
> Julie is the coal car, oh yes."

"Mary wore a red dress" becomes

> "Anyone wearing a red dress (blue socks)
> Wash up for lunch."

"Bye-o-baby, bye" ("The Mail Boat," #6) can help children settle down if sung

"Bye-o-baby, bye. Bye-o-baby, bye.
Now Jenny is resting."

You can use the children's names in the form of an "attendance song." At one of the early sessions you can begin by singing to the tune of "Did You Ever See a Lassie?" (#11), "Did you know my name is Peggy, is Peggy, is Peggy? And what is your name?"—using your own name in the first line. Address this question to a child who you think will respond. He in turn must choose another child. Besides being fun, this will help the children learn each other's names.

PART SINGING

Rounds are too difficult for preschoolers, but part singing of a sort is possible. Choose question and answer songs like "Did You Go To the Barney?" (#9), "Oh, John, the Rabbit" (#9), or "Who Did?" (#11). Sing the question and have the children sing the answer. Later you can divide the children into a questioning and an answering group. Songs with an echo effect like "By'm Bye" (#11), or "Train is A-coming" (#9) can be used the same way. In a song like "Frog Went A' Courting" (#11) let the children make up the noises for you to repeat. Another way to divide a song is to have one group of children (or even a soloist) sing the verse of a song, while the rest join in for the chorus. "Fire Down Below" (#9) or "Pick a Bale of Cotton (#9) are two examples of songs with clear-cut verse and chorus.

MADE-UP SONGS

Children do a lot of spontaneous singing. They don't care whether it is special singing time or not. They sing songs that they know, or they make up songs of their own. If you take these songs seriously—by not laughing at them, or by picking up what they are singing and singing back to them—you encourage further experimentation.

Some songs children make up are really good, and you may want to take them down. The children will love this. You can write down the words, if nothing else, and the words will remind you of the tune. If you can write musical notes, all the better. If you can't, a simple way to record music is to use numbers. Call middle C one, D two, E three and so on, until C above middle C becomes eight. Toy xylophones and their music are numbered in precisely this way.

ACCOMPANIMENT

It is not necessary to buy an accompanying instrument if you don't already have one. It doesn't make too much difference for the kind of singing you do with preschoolers. Even if you have a piano, chances are that it isn't in the playroom where most of the spontaneous singing goes on. A guitar is better, if you play one, because it can be taken to the playroom and you don't have to sit with your back to the children while you play it. If you play neither piano nor guitar, but feel strongly about the need for an accompanying instrument, you can buy an autoharp. It is easy to carry and costs less than $50. You can teach yourself to strum a few chords very quickly and easily, without the dexterity necessary to learn even elementary guitar chords.

SINGING GAMES

A large number of children's songs have actions to go with the words. Most of them are simply imitative games—"Do as I Do." Be sure to keep your focus on whether the kids are having fun and not on how strictly they're following the rules.

The following is a list of action songs good for playgroups.

"Looby Loo" (#11)
"Hokey Pokey" (#11)
"Ring Around the Rosey" (#7)
"Pop Goes the Weasel" (#11)
"Put Your Finger in the Air" (#11)
"Clap, Clap, Clap Your Hands" (#9)
"The Mulberry Bush" (#11)
"Oats, Peas, Beans and Barley Grow" (#11)
"Up On the Mountain" (#6)
"Did You Ever See a Lassie?" (#11)
"Come on and Join into the Game" (#11)

Many of these can have new actions substituted for the original ones. "Clap, Clap, Clap Your Hands" can be played "Stamp Your Feet" or "Tap Your Knee." "This is the way the bunny hops" or "This is the way the turtle crawls" or "This is the way the lion stalks" can be sung and acted to the tune of "Mulberry Bush."

Others were composed to allow improvisations. "Up On the Mountain," "Did You Ever See a Lassie?" and "Come on and Join into the Game" are standards of this type.

Many songs become action songs if the children act out the words. "The Fox" (#11), "Bought Me a Cat" (#9) and "Jack and Jill" (#2) are only three of many songs suitable for acting out.

Dramatizing to music

WHAT TO DRAMATIZE

Any experience familiar to all the children can provide a theme for dramatization. You can start with a broad statement like "What I like to do in the snow," or "How I help my Mommy," or "At the playground." A street being repaired or a fire in the neighborhood provides new material for this activity.

Tell the children that you are going to play "snow" music and that as you play, they are to pretend that they are out in the snow doing something they like to do.

The themes can be based on a trip the children have taken. The day after the children have been to the zoo, ask them to think about some animal they liked. Play some music for them and let them act out being the animal.

Your beginning themes may have to be more specific. Children adore being mice who come out to scamper about (quick, staccato music) until the cat comes (slow, heavy chords) and they must scurry to their holes. As you might imagine, any very simple animal themes of this nature are usually well received.

ACCOMPANYING DRAMATIZATION

For mothers who are not experienced pianists, but who read music adequately, many of the song collections at the end of this chapter will provide music of as many tempos and moods as you might need. Some even suggest themes for dramatization. There are music books which are written for the specific purpose of providing music for accompanying children's dramatizations and movements, like (#4, 7).

If you don't read music very well, you can probably do an adequate job of accompanying the children. You can use the one or two pieces you still remember from past piano lessons or learn one or two new pieces. It's better to know them by heart so that you won't have to keep your eyes on the keyboard, but will be able to watch the children. Practice playing these pieces at various tempos, staccato, legato, and on different parts of the keyboard. You will learn how these different variations are suited to various themes. If you've never taken piano lessons, try to see how many different ways you can learn to play "Chopsticks."

Experiment with the piano to find different effects you can use. Here are a few suggestions:

- A scale is readily accepted as walking music.
- Chords in the bass can be papa bear walking, a lion roaring, a tiger stalking.
- Playing a scale—each note played twice, the second note played staccato—is good skipping music.
- Any chord played at jumping tempo becomes jumping music.
- A run of three notes, or an arpeggio played repeatedly, can be used as running music.
- Sliding your thumb down a scale for about an octave is good sliding music.
- A C chord in the octave above middle C, alternated with the C chord at middle C, can be a see-saw or a swing.
- A soft, mildly staccato chord repeated regularly can be a slow, steady rain, while a fast alternation of a black key and the white key above it can become a fast spring rain.

Dancing

Children can respond to music even when no themes have been presented. They are the original interpretive dancers, unless you meet the occasional young child who has been encouraged to Twist or Frug because it is so "cute." With encouragement from you, even he can begin to relax and become more natural. Children of three and four are in the midst of finding out who they are and what they can do. Free dancing helps them find out what they are capable of.

The first time you try dancing, tell the children you are going to play some music you think they will enjoy dancing to. Suggest that they listen first, and when they feel like moving they can begin. The greater variety of music you present, the better. Be sure to include music of all moods and tempos.

ACCOMPANYING DANCING

Whether you play well enough to accompany children's dancing or use phonograph records, there is a great variety of music to choose from. Brahms, Liszt, Tchaikovsky, De Falla, Bartok, Johann Strauss and Saint Saëns are just a few of the classical musicians whose danceable music is available as sheet music or on records. There is also much ethnic dance music available in books and on records. If you have no records of your own, you will find that one well-chosen folk dance record will go a long way. If you care to buy more, all the better.

PROPS

There are some props which can be used to help children move more freely. These props by their very nature encourage children to explore the space around them, helping them to move from one spot on the floor, and encouraging them to move their hands.

Nylon or thin chiffon scarves. They flutter and billow and pull, and the child follows along.

Lengths of brightly colored crepe-paper streamers. You might tape long strips of these streamers to the end of a piece of doweling for a dance shaker.

Large balls (at least 8″–10″ in diameter) to be bounced or tossed to the music. The youngest children can roll them to each other.

Christmas bells strung on elastic, to be worn on the wrist or ankle. These can accompany the children's movements, leaving the hands free for dancing. Some teething rings have bells and are large enough to be worn bracelet fashion.

Hoops. Raised above the head, they make children feel taller. Children can roll them along the floor—without letting go—to various tempos. Held at the top and tapped on the floor at the bottom, they become percussion instruments. Laid on the floor, hoops are houses for mice to scamper in and out of, beds for children to curl up in during a lullabye, boats to row, or anything else you or the children can imagine.

Rhythms

The rhythm of a piece of music is the first thing children respond to. With the use of rhythm instruments they can experiment with the beat of a piece of music and the various kinds of sounds that instruments make. They can dance to rhythm instruments alone—without accompaniment from a piano or a record. Even clapping hands and stamping feet can be used as rhythm instruments.

Every playgroup mother should have a number of rhythm instruments available for the children, whether or not she feels that she wants to have organized rhythm activities. There are many things children can find out about rhythms and rhythm instruments on their own if the instruments are accessible.

Planned rhythm activities should be offered periodically at one or two homes. If none of the mothers owns a good drum with a real skin head, one should be bought by the mothers as a group, and it can be passed around as it is needed.

RHYTHM INSTRUMENTS

What instruments you buy and how many depends on your budget and how well you can improvise. Try to provide an assortment of instruments: drums, ringing instruments, all-wood instruments, shakers. Whatever you buy or make, let the individual pieces have as good a tone quality as possible. Here are a few ideas on instruments you can buy or make.

DRUMS

Provide a variety of drums, if possible. Many kinds are available on the market. They may be small and inexpensive, or they may be very large and out of the financial reach of most playgroups. Small inexpensive ones that are readily available are made in Japan and have a pair of bells attached to them. Better drums are being imported from Korea.

Whatever you do, don't buy the fancy drums with cardboard skins sold in many toy departments. Considering that they are easily broken and that they generally don't have a good tone, they are very expensive. An oatmeal box will serve as well.

Home-made Drums

Buy a drum head skin at an instrument repair shop and attach it to a nail keg, a wooden flower pot, a large chopping bowl, or whatever wooden barrel or bucket you can find. First soak the skin in cold water for ten to fifteen minutes. When it is soft and pliable, squeeze it out and stretch it across the top of the barrel, attaching it to the top of the barrel sides with upholstery nails. Hammer in a nail on one side while pulling the skin directly opposite. Turn the drum a quarter turn and repeat the process. Continue in this way until the skin is firmly attached.

Open both ends of some coffee cans (one-pound and two-pound sizes). Cover the ends with plastic coffee-can lids. For variation, punch holes in the edge of the lid and string Christmas bells through each individual hole before putting the lid on the can.

A piece of inner tube can be stretched over the top of a large can and held on with several windings of stout cord or additional strips of inner tube.

Heavy plastic, chamois (soaked first) and parchment are other materials that can be used for drum heads. Spray them with spray shellac for added stiffness and better tone.

Wooden kitchen spoons, chopsticks, and wooden mallets that come with children's peg sets make satisfactory drum and gong sticks.

For some of your drums and gongs you will want softhead drumsticks. To make these, buy the small replacement balls that

are sold (two to a pack) for use with paddles. Insert a thin
(¼") 12"-long dowel into the ball after poking a hole into it
and filling it with glue.

BELLS

Indian bells, often available at the five-and-ten. Children can
hold them in their hands to ring them, or strike them when they
are suspended from a rod by string.

Cowbells.

Wrist bells. You can buy teething rings with bells that sell for
about fifteen cents, or you can sew Christmas bells to a bracelet
of 1" elastic, using coat thread.

Triangles.

A juice-can bell. Punch a hole in the bottom of a large juice
can, turn it upsidedown and thread it with a string. Tie a large
knot at the end of the string inside the can to keep it from
slipping. Tie the other end to a rod. When struck, the can sounds
like a bell.

Plumbing-pipe bells. Buy some lengths of pipe (no shorter
than 12") at a plumbing supply store. Have two holes drilled
opposite each other at one end, run heavy cord through the
holes, and suspend the pipes from a rod. The tone and pitch of
these pipes when struck will depend on the diameter and length,
as well as the composition.

TONE BLOCKS

Real Mexican *claves*. You cannot duplicate their tone with a
substitute.

Two building blocks to be struck on the floor or on each other.

Two pieces of wood covered with rough sandpaper, to make
sand blocks that can be hit or scraped. You can screw drawer-pulls
to the backs, to make them easier to handle.

Rhythm sticks. These can be made from 9" lengths of thick
doweling, but you may prefer to buy them because they need to
be sealed with many layers of paint or other sealer for the best
effect. Hardwood dowels sound better than softwood dowels.

Lengths of wood of different kinds and thicknesses, suspended
from a rod and struck.

GONGS

A pie tin or a pot lid becomes a gong when a hole is punched at one edge of it (with a large nail or a drill), and it is suspended from a rod by string.

Some pots make excellent gongs. Experiment with yours to find the ones with the best tones.

RATTLES

Mexican *maracas*. Rattles made by filling containers with rice, sand, dried beans or peas, or bottle caps. The children will enjoy making their own.

Bouillon-cube tins, metal holders for individual cigars, sour-cream or yogurt containers, pill vials, small pastille tins, movie-film canisters, 35mm-film canisters, paper cups for hot drinks (stapled shut), and brown paper bags can all be filled and converted to rattles.

TAMBOURINES

Try to avoid five-and-ten-cent store tambourines, if possible. They generally have poor sound quality. A good wood and parchment tambourine is not very expensive. The coffee-can drum with the bells attached (see Drums) is a better substitute.

OTHERS

Kazoos, whistles, clickers, toy xylophones or anything else can be used if the tone is good—that is, neither harsh nor tinny. This often has no relation to price.

SUSPENDING INSTRUMENTS

If you have a doorway chinning bar, you already have a bar from which to suspend instruments. If not, measure the width of your doorway and cut a piece of 1″ doweling so that it is ⅝″ shorter than the width of your door. Attach rubber chair tips (sometimes called crutch tips) to each end, and you will find that the rod fits tightly into the doorway. Cut crosswise grooves in the top of the rod, or nail in some wood staples (but don't nail them absolutely flat) to keep the suspending cords in place. Three instruments at a time are enough for an ordinary doorway. Adjust the bar so that the instruments hang at the children's arm level.

Introducing rhythm instruments

For introducing rhythm instruments, choose a song that has an especially strong beat and which the children already know, such as "I've Been Working on the Railroad," "When the Saints Come Marching In" (#1), "She'll Be Coming Around the Mountain." Tell them to sing and march to the song. Next, instead of marching, tell them to clap their hands at each place they would have stepped. Now give them rhythm instruments. If possible, give them all the same instruments to avoid fighting, or at least give out only two kinds that can later be exchanged. (Introduce the instruments slowly—one or two kinds at a session.) Tell the children that they are to play the instruments when they would have clapped.

Using rhythm instruments

There is no right or wrong way to play a rhythm instrument, unless the child is doing something destructive. There are many things children can find out by trying instruments in other than the conventional ways.

Don't get upset if some children have trouble keeping time. Keeping time improves with age, as does coordination.

- Direct different instruments or the entire ensemble, or let one of the children do it after they have observed you.
- Use rhythm instruments without accompaniment. For example, ask one child to walk in front of the other children. "Close your eyes and listen for when John's feet touch the

ground. Now open your eyes and see if we can clap every time John's feet touch the ground." This can be followed by an instrumental accompaniment to the rhythm of John's feet. Susie will move a different way, and the whole process can be repeated.

- Ask one child to walk like a Daddy or a Mommy, and have the children beat out that rhythm. Ask another child to walk as he always does (like a child). This will sound quite different, of course. Then ask the two children to walk together and assign the remaining children to accompany one child while you accompany the other. Other combinations can be used, too. A hurried walk can be paired with a tired walk. A cowboy could be paired with a sailor, and so on. This activity is for the older playgroupers.
- Have the children do "what the drum tells you to do." They can walk, skip, hop or run as the drum beats out appropriate rhythms. The drum beats can be loud or soft and the children can tell whether they are to tiptoe or not depending on the loudness of the tapping.
- Beat the rhythm of a child's name on a drum to take attendance. Children love to try to recognize their own names this way, and often get very good at identifying other names: MIK-ey, Su-ZANNE, Di-ANN-a.
- Play "Talking Drums." "Speak" to a child by tapping a simple rhythm (like / /, or '' /) on your drum. Tell him that to answer you, he must tap the same message on his drum, tone blocks, or by clapping his hands.

As instruments are introduced, they should go into an instrument box or basket that is available to the children at all times. You will find that this does *not* lead to chaotic playing of loud music.

Developing concepts through music

- When children "Do what the music tells you to," whether the music comes from a piano, record or even a rhythm instrument, they start listening for fast-slow, loud-soft qualities of music as well as for all the various rhythm combinations.

- In a rudimentary way they become aware of the counting value of different kinds of notes. A game like "Talking Drums" or a song like "The Clocks" (#7) is particularly helpful.
- Children can get an idea of high-low in music when pretending to swing or seesaw, if you alternate a C chord in the upper part of the piano with a C chord in the bass. They can chant "high," "low," or "up," "down," as they are doing it.
- Records like "Peter and the Wolf" and Benjamin Britten's "Young Person's Guide to the Orchestra" (#33) introduce children to the many instruments. Anyone who can come and play an instrument for the playgroup increases the children's knowledge.
  The children like to see pictures of the instruments they have heard, try to listen for the "trumpet" or the "violin" on another record later.
- With free access to drums children can learn that:
  A drum sounds different in the middle than at the edges.
  A drum sounds different if hit by a softheaded stick, a plain stick, a whisk, or with the hand.
  A handful of rice on the drum head shows children that the drum head moves when it is hit.
- Free access to all kinds of instruments allows children to find out that:
  Rattles sound different when filled with small things than when filled with large ones.
  Bells, triangles and ringing instruments sound different when held than when hanging free.
  There are many different ways to make sounds with any instrument.
- Children feel the emotional impact of music. Play a happy piece, but do not identify it as such. Do the children think it is happy or sad? Is it fast or slow?
  Play a sad piece. Is it happy or sad? Is it fast or slow?
  Play another slow piece which is not sad, to show the children that all slow pieces are not sad.
- Is it music? Read the children a nursery rhyme or poem that has been set to music, like "Who Has Seen the Wind?" (#7). Now sing the same rhyme or poem.

Which time did you make music? What is the difference between when you said the words and when you sang them?

Song and music books

1—Bailey, Charity (ed.), *Sing a Song*, Plymouth Music Co., N. Y.
2—Bertail, Inez (ed.), *Complete Nursery Song Book*, Lothrop, N. Y.
3—Boni, Margaret (ed.), *Fireside Book of Folk Songs*, Simon & Schuster, N. Y.
4—Buttolph, Edna G., *Music Is Motion*, Willis Music Co., Cincinnati, Ohio.
5—Coleman, Satis N. and Thorn, Alice G., *Singing Time*, John Day Co., N. Y.
6—Landeck, Beatrice (ed.), *Songs to Grow On*, Edward Marks Music Publishers-William Sloane, N. Y.
7—MacCarteney, Laura P., *Songs for the Nursery School*, Willis Music Co., Cincinnati, Ohio.
8—Miller, Mary and Zajan, Paula (Collectors), *Finger Play*, G. Schirmer, N. Y.
9—Seeger, Ruth Crawford (ed.), *American Folk Songs for Children*, Doubleday, Garden City, N. Y.
10—Seeger, Ruth Crawford (ed.), *Animal Folk Songs for Children*, Doubleday, Garden City, N. Y.
11—Winn, Marie (ed.), *Fireside Book of Children's Songs*, Simon & Schuster, N. Y.

Some suggested children's records

12—*Activity Songs for Kids*	Marcia Berman	Folkways	FC	7023
13—*American Folk Songs for Children*	Pete Seeger	"	FC	7001
14—*American Game and Activity Songs*	Pete Seeger	"	FC	7002
15—*Animals, Vol. 1*	Alan Mills	"	FC	7021
16—*The Baby Sitter's Family Album*	The Baby Sitters	Vanguard	VRS	9173
17—*Birds, Beasts, Bugs and Bigger Fish*	Pete Seeger	Folkways	FC	7011
18—*Birds, Beasts, Bugs and Little Fish*	Pete Seeger	"	FC	7010
19—*Children's Concert*	Oscar Brand	Wonderland		1438
20—*Children's Concert*	Tom Glazer	"		1452

21—*Children's Songs and Games from the Southern Mountains*	Jean Ritchie	Folkways	FC	7054
22—*Counting Games and Rhythms for Little Ones*	Ella Jenkins	Folkways	FC	7056
23—*Ding-Dong School Singing Games*	Miss Frances Mitch Miller	Golden	GLP	49
24—*Folksongs by the Baby Sitters*	Baby Sitters	Vanguard	VRS	9042
25—*French Folk Songs for Children*	Alan Mills	Folkways	FC	7208
26—*Little White Duck and Other Songs*	Burl Ives	Columbia	HL	9507
27—*March Along*		Wonderland		1486
28—*Merry-Go-Round of Children's Songs*	Bonnie Dobson	Prestige	Int	13064
29—*More Animals, Vol. 2*	Alan Mills	Folkways	FC	7022
30—*More Songs to Grow On*	Alan Mills	"	FC	7009
31—*Musical Mother Goose*		Golden	LP	65
32—*Nursery Rhymes, Games and Folk Songs*	Cisco Houston	Folkways	FC	7006
33—*Peter and the Wolf and Young Person's Guide to the Orchestra*	Brandon de Wilde, Narrator	VOX	PL	9280
34—*Sing a Song of Childhood*	Marjorie Bennett	Wonderland		3028
35—*Sing a Song with Charity Bailey*	Charity Bailey	Decca	K	155
36—*Song and Play Time with Pete Seeger*	Pete Seeger	Folkways	FC	7526
37—*Songs and Fun with the Baby Sitters*	Baby Sitters	Vanguard	VRS	9053
38—*Songs in French for Children*	Lucienne Vernay	Columbia	CL	675
39—*Songs to Grow On*	Woody Guthrie	Folkways	FC	7005
40—*Tom Glazer's Second Concert*	Tom Glazer	Battle		6601
41—*Train to the Zoo*		Children's Record Guild		1001
42—*Whoever Shall Have Some Peanuts*	Sam Hinton	Folkways	FC	7530
43—*Winnie the Pooh*	Jack Gilford	Golden	LP	95

CHAPTER 9

Science

FOR most of the first two years of his life, the young child is involved in touching, tasting, smelling, looking, listening. But the more he can learn in a second-hand way, through words as his language and understanding improve, the less he is encouraged to learn directly. By the time they have reached school many children lose much of the curiosity about the world around them.

This curiosity—Why? How? Who? Where? When? How can I find out?—is the basic outlook of the scientist. The science part of your playgroup program helps children keep and develop this basic curiosity; helps them observe as well as see, listen as well as hear. In the process, both you and the children will have a lot of fun. If children are encouraged to look at things questioningly, everything around them will have more meaning for the rest of their lives.

There are specific science activities you can do with your playgroup. Other ideas will arise from other activities the children are involved in. This chapter suggests a number of specific activities. They in turn will suggest still others to you. A number of guide questions have been listed with each activity. You know your playgroup, so you are the best judge of which questions will be the most meaningful to your children, and how many you can ask at any one time. The children will set the pace. Also, keep in mind that the age of your children very definitely helps to determine how much they will get from each activity. Learning science is a slow process, built step by step.

Science equipment

• At least one good U-shaped or horseshoe magnet and several cheap ones. Bar magnets are harder for children to hold and have more parts to get lost.

• A magnifying glass. A nice addition is a tripod magnifier which can be set down, and is not subject to the same shaking that happens when a child tries to hold a magnifying glass still. These are available in many hobby shops for around $1.

• One or two pulleys. These can be bought at any housewares store. Film reels can serve as substitutes.

• A flashlight.

Science in the kitchen

You don't have to be a scientist yourself to help young children with science. Every time you go into the kitchen to cook, you are dealing with scientific principles.

COOKING AND BAKING

Stoves are too high for little children. For many of these activities, you will find it helpful to do the cooking in an electric fry pan or on a hot plate put on top of an asbestos pad—either one placed on a lower table. The children can participate more and watch changes better at this height.

Powdered Drinks

Children love the fruit-flavored drinks that are made by dissolving flavored sugar in water. What easier way is there to introduce the concept of *solutions?* Don't be afraid to use words like *dissolve* and *solution*. Children often learn them as easily as other words, and using proper terms keeps you from having to talk around an idea in order to talk about it.

What happened to the orange powder?

Do you think we could take the orange powder out again by pouring the drink through a strainer? (Try it.)

Taste the plain water. Does it have a taste?
Taste the drink. What gave the water its taste?

Smell the water. Does it have a smell?
Smell the drink. What gave the water its smell?

Look at the water. Does it have a color?
Look at the drink. What gave the water its color?

Gelatine Desserts

By making gelatine desserts with the children, you can carry their concept of solutions even further. Make two packages of gelatine, dissolving one in hot water and the other in cold.

What is at the bottom of this bowl? (Dissolved in cold water.)
Is there any (or as much) gelatine at the bottom of this bowl? (Dissolved in hot water.)

What kind of water helps things dissolve better?

Cocoa

Cocoa is a favorite drink on a cold winter day. When the children make it, they can see the cocoa dissolving in the hot water (or milk).

Fruit Salad

If children help make a fresh fruit salad for their lunch, they have a wonderful opportunity to observe the parts of fruits. If you are right there, they can peel and core them, cut them into small pieces, and in general, learn to work a number of kitchen utensils. If none of the children is allergic to nuts, nuts can be cracked and added to the salad.

You can buy fruit beforehand, of course. But it is even better to take the children shopping for it.

Applesauce

Most children love to eat applesauce, so it is fun for them to make it as well. In preparing it, they have a chance to peel, core and slice. They can puree the apples by passing them through a strainer or through a food mill.

Does the applesauce look the same as the apple in the top of the mill?

Why is the applesauce smoother than this apple (in the mill)?

Why didn't all of the apple go through the holes?

Vegetable Soup

Another recipe that allows the children a good opportunity to use utensils is vegetable soup. Even if your child doesn't ordinarily eat it, you may find that he is keen to try a soup he has helped make.

Set aside some of the raw vegetables and a piece of raw meat so that the children can compare the raw with the cooked.

What happened to the vegetables?

What do you think made them softer?

Soupmaking usually involves many hours' cooking, so you will have to make it in a pressure cooker. Cook a small amount of soup in an ordinary pot.

Which soup got done?

Which pot was more tightly closed?

What happened when I ran cold water on the pressure cooker?

Playdough

Making playdough (Chapter 7) teaches children a number of things about science, in addition to giving them an art material. They feel the difference between the salt and the flour as they add them to the mixture and as they knead the ingredients together.

How does the salt feel?

How does the flour feel?

Look at the salt as you pour it. Look at the flour as you pour it. Do they pour the same?

Why do you think they feel different?

Why do you think they pour differently?

What is happening to the salt and the flour as you mix them?

Can you show the salt part? the flour part?

How does the playdough feel? like the flour? like the salt?

Do you think it would be easy to take out the salt? the flour? the water from the playdough?

Let the children look at the salt and the flour under a magnifying glass.

Cupcakes, Muffins, and Other Quickbreads

When making cupcakes and quickbreads, children can learn that things seem to change when they are mixed with other things, dissolving things in water changes their texture, and baking changes things even further.

You can begin by using a package mix, but interesting and important steps are skipped when you use a mix, because they have already been done at the factory. And besides, nothing tastes better than baked goods made from scratch.

To make mixing dough easier for children, let the butter get to room temperature before you begin, and use pre-sifted flour. On the other hand, let them sift their own flour occasionally, and have them feel it before and after sifting. If you have used several cups of flour, it is possible to show the children how much greater volume the sifted flour takes than does the unsifted flour you started with.

Butter

All you need to make butter is heavy cream at room temperature and a tight-fitting jar with a couple of marbles in it.

Let the children take turns shaking the cream up and down until the butter begins to form. This method is most like the old butter churns. Do not expect all the butter fat to turn to butter in the time the children will be willing to spend in shaking. You can also make butter by beating the cream with a rotary egg beater. When you have as much butter as you want, separate the butter from the remaining milk by using a cheesecloth strainer. Rinse the butter in cold water.

Let the children taste some heavy cream you have set aside, and compare it with the milk that was poured off.

Do these two things taste the same?

What did we do that made the difference?

If the children are unaccustomed to unsalted butter, give them a little bit of commercial salted butter to compare with it, and ask them what difference they notice.

Virginia Kahl's *Away Went Wolfgang* and "The King's Breakfast" from Milne's *When We Were Very Young* are appropriate to read the day you make butter. There are other stories and poems that go with many of the other science activities, too.

Cottage Cheese

Most little children have no idea that the refrigerator keeps food from spoiling. They know only that it keeps things cold. Ask your playgroup children what they think would happen to milk if it were not kept in the refrigerator.

Keep the milk in a covered container in a warm (*not* hot) place. You will see the curds separating from the whey when the cheese is ready. Separate them by using a bag made by gathering the edges of a clean linen towel. Squeeze the cheese even after it has stopped draining by itself.

Let the children compare the smell, taste and consistency of milk that has been refrigerated, and this milk that has not.

Raisins

Refrigeration is only one technique used to retard spoilage. Raisins—almost all youngsters love them—are examples of foods that have been preserved by drying.

Put some grapes in a sunny window, covered with cheesecloth to keep out dirt and soot. Spread the grapes out and turn them periodically until you have raisins. You can use different kinds of grapes or currants.

Leave a bunch of grapes of the same size in your refrigerator or in a dish away from the sun, so that the children can make a comparison and actually observe what the sun does to fruit.

Pumpkin Seeds

At Halloween, if you make a Jack O'Lantern with the children, save the seeds and dry them in a slow oven on a greased cookie sheet. Turn them and salt them. In many places these seeds are packaged and sold to be eaten.

Eat them.

Compare them with some seeds that were not dried.

Plant a few baked seeds and a few untouched seeds. Which ones grew? Why?

Before you throw away the Jack O'Lantern, cut off a piece and save it. Let the children smell it.

Does this piece of pumpkin smell like the fresh pumpkin?

Is the smell stronger near the green places (or black, depending on what kind of mold has begun to grow)?

Let the children look at the mold through a magnifying glass.

Cranberry Sauce

Thanksgiving time suggests making cranberry sauce. The children enjoy washing, cleaning and measuring the berries. They watch the sugar dissolve. It is fun for them to see and hear the berries pop as they get cooked.

Why do the berries pop?

Do they look the same after they have been cooked?

Do they feel the same?

Other Cooking Suggestions

- Christmas cookies decorated with confectioner's-sugar icing
- Cherry tarts for Washington's birthday
- Freshly squeezed orange juice. (Your playgroup children may believe that orange juice comes from cans, not oranges)
- Lemonade, starting with fresh lemons
- Popcorn
- Candy, using recipes on dry cereal boxes
- Puddings

CANDLES

Candle dipping is fun at Christmas or Chanukah, or just any old time. Melt some household paraffin (available at the grocery store) in a coffee can set in a container of water. *Do not* have the container of wax directly on the heat. To make colored candles, melt scraps of wax crayons with the paraffin. When the paraffin has melted, remove the double boiler from the heat.

Use long strings for wicks. Thumbtack each to an end of a dowel or to the stiff cardboard tube sometimes found on wire hangers. Each child holds on to a dowel or tube, and dips the wick as though he were fishing. He must dip in and out quickly

or the wax on the wick will remelt. If you line up the children
and let each one dip, and then send him to the end of the line,
you will minimize any possible accidents and also give the wax
a chance to harden. Layers of wax are built up this way, and the
candle is ready when it is as fat as the child wants it to be. If
the wax in the coffee can thickens too much, place the double
boiler back on the heat.

What happened to the pieces of wax we put in the can?

What do you think made the wax *melt* into a *liquid?*

What made the *liquid* wax start thickening into a *solid* again?

USING KITCHEN IMPLEMENTS

Can Opener

Opening a can of juice to be used for snacktime can demonstrate a scientific principle. Use a beer-can opener and punch a
small hole on only one side of the can top. Pour juice. Punch
another hole in the can top, and pour again.

What happened when I poured juice through the first hole?

What was different when I poured juice the second time?

Do you know what helped push the juice out after I made
the second hole?

A wall can opener is exciting for the children to use, and is
just one of many wheels and axles to be found around the house.

Rotary Egg Beater

Plan to make scrambled eggs for lunch one day. Let the children beat their own eggs, using a fork, a wire whisk and a
rotary beater.

Which of these beat the eggs the best?

Why do you think it worked the best?

Can you think of any other wheels that help us?

Growing plants

Growing plants is great fun for children. They rarely fail to
get excited when they see the first shoot emerging where before
there was only a seed. There are so many varieties of seeds and

mature plants, that the possibilities for learning are limitless.

Plants can be grown in pots, in cut-down milk cartons with holes at the bottom, in windowboxes, and if you have a yard, in a plot that you can call the Playgroup Garden.

KITCHEN CUTTINGS AND SEEDS

Your kitchen can supply you with many of the seeds and plants that you and the children may want to grow.

Carrots, Turnips and Other Roots

Chop off all but an inch of carrot and trim off all but an inch of the greens. Take the vegetable containing both carrot and greens and place in a shallow dish of water, carrot-side down. The greens will begin to sprout anew in a week or two, and it may blossom, although no new carrots will grow.

Onions

You have had the experience of having an onion sprout when it was kept in a warm place and the weather was humid. To make an onion sprout, place the onion on the rim of a jar of water, root part down and touching the water. If it is kept in a dark, warm place, it will begin to sprout in a few days.

Yams, Sweet Potatoes and Other Tubers

Yams and sweet potatoes develop long vines, as do white potatoes. Put one end of your tuber into a jar of water, and keep it in a warm, dark place until the sprouting begins.

. In cities that have a large Latin-American population, you can find a number of more exotic tubers, such as the Yautía, which sprout into interesting plants.

If you have a Playgroup Garden, try cutting a potato into sections—an eye to a section—and planting them.

Avocado

Avocados (or alligator pears) develop into tall plants, once started. Place the seed flat end down in a jar of water; once the roots begin to grow, they must be planted in soil. Only the end should touch the water, so you may want to support the seed by pushing a toothpick into each of three sides, and rest the toothpicks on the lip of the jar. Pinch back the plants once they are about 9 inches high, to make them lusher and less spindly.

Pineapples

Pineapples can be grown in much the same way as carrots— by having the top inch of the plant and the greens cut from the whole pineapples. It is a good idea to dry it for a few days, as the pineapple meat sometimes rots otherwise. This top section can then be rooted by being placed on the lip of a jar of water, with only the actual pineapple touching the water. You may need to use toothpick supports.

Fruit and Vegetable Seeds

Children can bring the seeds of fruits and vegetables they ate at home, or you can save them from cooking activities such as applesauce, fruit salad, pumpkin pie, or vegetable soup.

Seeds often germinate better if they are soaked first.

Dried Peas and Beans

If you want quick results, plant some of the dried beans (lima, navy or kidney) or peas that you probably have on hand. You will get plants in a matter of days.

Bulbs

If you have a garden, you can plant any variety of bulb easily. Plant it in the fall, and it will bloom in the spring.

Onions are bulbs, but they are not flowering plants. Two easily grown flowering bulbs are the hyacinth and the narcissus.

Plant the small hyacinth bulbs, one to a pot, in small pots. Water them well and put them in plastic bags or in plastic wrap, leaving an air space of about two inches above the pot. Seal the bag closed. Keep the bulbs in a very cold—but not freezing—place. If you need to, use the bottom shelf of your refrigerator. In about a month's time you will have hyacinths.

The narcissus can be *forced* to bloom in about two months. Cover the bottom of a dish with pebbles or pearl chips sold for fish tanks. Put in several bulbs, half covering them with more pebbles. Use just enough water in the bowl to keep the bottom of the bulbs wet, and put the bulbs in a sunny place.

LOOKING AT SEEDS

Children can actually watch seeds *germinate*—if you put some dried beans into a small container lined with damp (not soggy) paper toweling, tissues or cotton. You can use the caps of large detergent bottles, half an egg shell, or cut-down milk cartons as containers.

• To show the germination of another kind of seed, follow the same procedure with some corn (or grass) seed. The bean has two seed leaves (cotyledons), the corn only one.

• You and the children will see the seed coat shrivel and fall off, as first the roots, and then the stem begin to emerge from the seed.

• You will see the plants grow toward the sun. Turn the plants around to show the children that they will again grow toward the sun.

• Plant some of the germinating seeds in soil. Leave some in water. Which ones eventually die?

• You can see the seed leaves shrivel and die as the true, food-making leaves develop.

Animals

Adults are so accustomed to domesticated animals that they sometimes forget that these animals are almost as exciting for young children as are the wild ones at the zoo or the museum.

PETS

Borrow a pet if you don't have one, or wangle an invitation from his owner if this is more practical. Prepare the children with some details about the particular animal. If you can also find an appropriate story—with pictures, if possible—it will prove helpful. A kitten, puppy, hamster, rabbit, bird, turtle, or any other kind of common animal can often be observed eating, cleaning himself, or playing, if the children try to be quiet.

Does he eat as we do?

Why can't he hold his food in his paws?

What are his ears like?

What color are his eyes?

How does he move? As we do?

UNUSUAL PETS

Aside from the usual pets, there are other animals that might be observed in the same way. Snakes, tadpoles and frogs, and various insects caught in nature are frequently kept at home. You and your playgroup might even catch such an animal on one of your field trips. (Chapter 14)

OTHER ANIMALS

Observing farm animals or animals in zoos is dealt with in Chapter 13.

Science in the house

PLUMBING

Children have only vague ideas about where their bath water comes from or where it goes. They are fascinated to follow pipes back from the spigot to the individual faucets and back into the wall. If you can, shut off the wall valve and show them that the water is no longer coming in. A trip to the basement will probably show the route of the incoming and outgoing pipes. Especially if you live in an apartment house, the children will be surprised to see how much fatter the pipes are in the basement than in the apartment.

ELECTRICITY

Children know that plugging things in and flipping switches "makes electricity work," but few of them know that electricity comes into their house with increasingly bigger wires. Show the children the wiring in your house. Show them the fuses or circuit breakers and shut off the electricity in one circuit (or in the whole house, if it won't make it too dark and frightening). Take the children to the basement and show them the meter.

Electric cables are hard to see, unless you come across a new cable being laid or an old one being replaced.

HEATING

Whatever kind of heating system your house has, there is a furnace involved. Take the children to see your furnace, or ask the superintendent of your building to let you see it. If it is an oil furnace, try to find out when the next supply will be delivered, and let the children see the oil being pumped from the truck into the basement. If it is a coal furnace, try to show the children the coal delivery.

Back in your house, hold a pinwheel or strips of cloth or paper just above the air vent or the radiator. Then hold it below the vent or the radiator.

How does the air feel up here?

Does it feel the same down here? How does it feel?

What do you think is making the pinwheel turn (strips flap upward)?

How do you think this room gets warm?

The telephone

The telephone is so important an item in any house, that no child reaches the age of three without being interested in it. Like so many other things, it is totally magic to him.

• Let the children listen to the dial tone.

• Dial your own number to get a busy signal. Are the two sounds the same?

• Begin to dial a number (the weather number, for example), and let the children listen to that. Do you hear anything?

• Complete the call. Let the children listen to the ringing

sound. Does it sound like the dial tone? Like the busy signal?

• Let them listen to the weather forecast for the day.

• On one of your walks, point out telephone poles and wires.

It is easy to make simple telephones that work. Take two paper cups ("hot cups" are the best) and punch a small hole in the end of each. Cut a length of string and thread its ends through the two holes—from the outside of the cup inward. Knot the ends of the string so it won't slip through the holes. The child who is the speaker covers his mouth with his cup and speaks into it. The child who is listening, covers his ear with his cup. For the telephone to work well, the string must be held straight.

The principle that explains the workings of this telephone is not the same one that explains the workings of the real telephone. But this simple device shows the children that telephones are connected by wires that transmit the sound in some way.

Science in the street

The streets in your neighborhood offer endless possibilities for scientific observations, such as:

• Observing that asphalt gets soft on hot days.

• Observing cement mixers, especially if you can see the ingredients going in first.

• Observing all kinds of pneumatic equipment used in street repairing.

• Observing the mechanisms involved in dump trucks and garbage trucks.

• Observing cranes with their pulleys, or a building painter on his scaffolding, also dependent on pulleys.

Some of the children may want to duplicate some of these things in their block building.

• Stores have merchandise delivered into their basements via sliding ramps, conveyor belts or even small elevators with visible pulleys.

• The streets are full of vehicles, all of which depend on wheels and axles.

Magnets

Magnets never fail to fascinate children. The cheap little magnets that are available at the dime store are all right if you also have at least one good one. By having a few different ones, the children can find out that magnets come in different strengths and that a strong one will pick up more than a weak one.

After the children have had an opportunity to try to pick up whatever strikes their fancy, give them a number of objects to try to pick up with your strongest magnet. Give them a box to put the attractable things in, and another for things that cannot be picked up. You can even mark one box "Yes" and the other one "No." Be sure that you include other metals besides iron or steel, so that the children get the idea that only some metals can be picked up with a magnet.

To keep your magnets in good shape, make sure that they are not dropped or banged on purpose. When they are put away, put a metal keeper, which comes with most magnets, or a large nail across the ends to keep the magnets from weakening.

Sensory games

There are a number of games for children that are not only fun, but that help sharpen their senses. Indeed some of these games are used in schools to prepare children for reading. Some can be played alone. Others need you and the entire playgroup. These games are so simple that you will be able to devise similar ones.

WHAT IS GONE?

Beginning with three objects, lay them out in a row in front of the children. Have them shut their eyes while you take away one object. They must open their eyes and tell you which object is gone.

As the children get better at the game, use more objects.

WHAT IS IT?

Take an object which has an obvious shape or texture, and hold
it on your lap under a towel or a piece of newspaper. You can
allow all the children except the child who is IT to see what
the object is. He must feel the object without looking at it, and
identify it. As the children get better at this game, the objects
can become more difficult, too. Begin with easy things like a
pencil, a spool, a piece of fur, a toothpick.

MATCH THE TEXTURE

Take six sheets of sandpaper of three different grades and
mount them separately on stiff cardboard. The object of the
game is to see whether the child who is playing the game can
match the three pairs by feel. Try to find sandpaper that has
the same background color regardless of grade, so that color
won't enter into the matching.

WHAT'S IN THE CAN?

Choose a few objects that make a characteristic sound when
shaken in a metal container. Show them to the children, and then
put them out of sight. Take one of the objects and shake it in
the container. Is it the metal screw? Is it the wooden spool? Is
it the rock? Is it the cloth?

MATCH THE SOUND

This game is similar to Match the Texture, but it is played
with sounds instead. Collect eight metal tubes—from bouillon or
cigars, for example. They should look identical. Divide them into
four pairs and fill each pair with identical objects: for example,
pair 1—marble; pair 2—a tablespoon of rice; pair 3—pieces of
gravel; pair 4—paper clips.

Introduce the game to the group as a whole. Call one child
at a time to you, give him a tube to shake and listen to, and have
him shake the others until he finds the one that makes the same
sound. Call a second child to find a second pair, and a third

child to find a third. "Do these two tubes that are left sound alike?" Take back the tubes and begin again to give your last child his turn.

This game can be played by one child by himself, too.

In this game, all the children have to hide their eyes. While their eyes are hidden, tiptoe to some section of the room and clap your hands, or ring a bell, or make some sound. Tiptoe away from that spot and tell the children that you are now "ready." They must tell you where you were on the basis of where they think the sound came from.

Other science concepts

You will find other science concepts throughout the book, for example, in the section on nature study in Chapter 13, in the discussion of floating in Chapter 16, in the discussion of colors in Chapter 7 and sound in Chapter 8.

CHAPTER 10

Stories and Poems

STORYTIME can be one of the most delightful and valuable periods of the playgroup morning. Books can help a young child understand himself and his relationships to other people better. They can reassure him about his strong feelings of anger, fear and jealousy by proving that all these feelings are universal. They can help prepare him for future experiences, both pleasant and unpleasant, such as having a new baby in the family, starting school, or going to the hospital. They can nourish his interest and liking for words and their sounds and meanings. Indeed, children like books for much the same reasons grownups do. One additional virtue of reading books to young children is that this activity, more than any other, encourages and prepares them to learn to read by themselves.

Choosing books for your playgroup

There is an enormous selection of children's books available today. Some are clearly marked for preschool children and others are not marked at all. How do you go about deciding whether a book is suitable for your playgroup, both in age level and in subject matter? Here are some general criteria for books for preschool children, as well as some specific suggestions for sub- to learn to read by themselves. The question becomes one of choosing the *right* books, for although there are many wonderful books written for children of this age, there are also many that are worthless.

GENERAL CHARACTERISTICS OF BOOKS FOR
PRESCHOOL CHILDREN

Style: clear and simple. Short sentences. Not many unfamiliar words. Not too long, taking into consideration young children's short attention span.

Contents: understandable, concrete ideas. One main character, generally, and a simple story line. Should include some familiar details, recognizable people, animals, relationships, feelings, in realistic stories as well as fantasy. Avoid themes that disturb preschoolers: abandonment or rejection by parents or key adults, frightening punishments, injury to the body.

Illustrations: for playgroup children, at least as important as the contents. Should be numerous, at least one illustration for each important idea in the story. Must be clear, and easily recognizable for what they are, with true, realistic colors, if color is used. Should add something to the story, either with touches of whimsey or extra details. Should be artistically appealing to you, tasteful and well executed.

GENERAL SUBJECTS THAT INTEREST PRESCHOOLERS

• Books about animals
• Books about families and feelings common to young children
• Books about transportation and machines
• Books about the changing weather, growing things, seasons
• Humorous books
• Books about what people do: policemen, firemen, mailmen, storekeepers, etc.

YOUR TASTE IS A DETERMINING FACTOR

If a child likes a particular book, it does not necessarily mean that this will be a good book to read to your playgroup. Your own like or dislike of the book is more important. Your taste has been developed over many years, and by your critical selection of books to read to children you will help them develop better standards of taste. A great number of badly written, sentimental, "cute" or banal books are available for children. Unfortunately, many of the low-priced books sold at the dime store fall into this category. These often include books about television characters, movie stars and even popular toys, as well as simplified versions of children's classics and various humorless books with heavy-handed morals. Many grownups feel no qualms about reading these books to children because they are readily available and because "the kids really like them." But children really like good books, too, and if presented with a steady diet of them, will eventually be able to recognize the inferior books for what they are and prefer to read the good ones.

STARTING OFF WITH TRIED AND TRUE FAVORITES

Your child surely has a few favorite books already that he cannot hear enough of and that conform to your standards of quality. The other children in the playgroup are not likely to know your child's particular favorites—there are too many books around. These tried and true favorites are good choices for your first few storytimes with your playgroup. As with all the other playgroup activities, the first time is most important and if the story you have selected falls flat, your chances for successful storytimes are greatly reduced. A time-tested favorite is not likely to fall flat. Your child will love to hear the story again with the other children around, and the fact that he likes it so much makes it probable that the other children will like it too. Your child will proudly show the other children his knowledge of the story by adding appropriate sound effects or prompting you when you stop for a word, and this will increase the other children's interest and curiosity about the story. After storytime has become a regular, popular part of your playgroup morning, you can try books that seem appealing to you and have not been tried out beforehand on your own child. There is a list of books particularly recommended for playgroups at the end of this chapter.

Reading to your playgroup

Although most children have had many stories read to them by the time they are three, listening to a story in a group is a somewhat different experience. The children are aware of each other and may find it harder to pay attention to the story than when they are alone with the reader. Their ability to listen attentively in a group will improve with time; it is important not to expect too much from them at first. If you see a child's attention beginning to wander, you can try to draw him back by saying his name, while reading the story: "And guess what happened then, Bobby? The dog ran away." Drawing attention to an interesting illustration may also bring back a distracted child. But if, at the beginning, you spend a great deal of time trying to get all the children to listen, they may get a resentful feeling about storytime and resist it from then on.

Find a comfortable place for storytelling, either on a large couch or on a rug, with the children on both sides of you. Make sure that they all can see the illustrations as you read. The children may like to be physically close to you during storytime, touching your arm or laying their heads in your lap. One child may like to snuggle right up *in* your lap. Let everybody get settled before you begin reading.

Be sure you have read the story once or twice before you read it to the group, and that you know it well enough to read in a conversational voice, looking up at the children as often as you can. Don't use a greatly inflected way of speaking and don't try for dramatic facial or vocal effects, especially the first few times. Read in a calm, natural voice, using tempo changes, if necessary, to add a little drama. Really dramatic, imitative reading is better for children a few years older than playgroup age; for very young children it is too distracting.

LETTING THE CHILDREN PARTICIPATE
IN YOUR READING

Whenever you select a story for your playgroup, read it over carefully with an eye for places where the children can participate in a simple way. If there is a repeated phrase that appears throughout the story, encourage the children to join in by pausing before you say some of the words: "A car that was old and a car that was _____," and the children will say "new." Animal sounds, train noises and various sound effects such as knocking or ringing a doorbell are other things children can do. If you wish, you can assemble a few simple props beforehand. There is a discussion about dramatizing stories in Chapter 15.

USING A FLANNELBOARD

A good way to make storytime less of a passive period is to use a flannelboard and cut-out pictures. You can buy a flannelboard and a complete set of flannel cutouts that includes most things you will need for your story, or you can make your own flannelboard. Paste a solid-colored piece of flannel on a large piece of cardboard or oaktag, on the top of a cardboard box, or on the backing of a large picture frame with the glass removed. When you have selected your story, cut out magazine pictures to illustrate it, or make your own. Glue a small strip of sandpaper or flannel to the back of each picture. When you are ready to read the story, give each child one or two of the cutouts and explain that when each hears his picture mentioned in the story, he is to take it to the flannelboard and press it on. As you read the story the first few times, you may have to remind the children of what they are to do: "A mother bird sat on her egg! . . . who has the mother bird?"

LOOKING AT THE ILLUSTRATIONS

As you read a story to your playgroup, give the children plenty of time to look at the illustrations before you turn each page. You can help the children develop their powers of observation by pointing out details in the illustration or asking them questions about what they see, but don't spend so long on an illustration that the children will lose track of the story.

Sometimes an illustration will seem to upset a child for no particular reason. He may close his eyes tightly, or seem to stare in strange fascination, or even begin to cry. Often the explanation lies in the child's ignorance of the laws of perspective. A child will worry about why a person shown in profile has only one eye, or why a partially obscured horse has only two feet. Children may also be upset by the absence, in an illustration, of a character mentioned in the story: "Where did the mother go?"

the child may ask, when only the children are shown in the picture. You will need to clear up these misconceptions and re-assure the children about the conventions of art as opposed to real things.

Poetry

Young children have a very basic enjoyment of the repetitions, alliterations and rhythmic patterns of poetry. Without the slightest encouragement, they will learn poetry by heart and proudly recite it to any willing listener. Unlike stories, which are usually reserved for a special storytime, poetry is best introduced in short doses at odd moments when it is suddenly appropriate: read "The Swing" after everybody has been swinging, "The Fog" on a foggy day, and so on.

NURSERY RHYMES

Nursery rhymes are an excellent introduction to poetry, and fortunately there are many colorfully illustrated books to choose from. Most nursery rhymes have traditional tunes that the children may already know. Indeed, children who have learned to sing a great number of nursery rhymes will invariably have a more musical approach to spoken poetry when introduced to it than children without this background. They will say the lines with greater inflections, emphasizing the rhymes and raising and lowering their voices appropriately, just as they did when singing the nursery rhymes.

FINGERPLAY POETRY

Fingerplay poetry invites active participation. Some have traditional music, and many have been passed on from generation to generation without losing their appeal. Because they are sometimes hard to find, eight popular fingerplays, with directions, are included below.

Open Them Shut Them

Open them, shut them, open them, shut them,
Give a little clap.

Open them, shut them, open them, shut them,
Lay them in your lap.
Creep them, creep them, creep them, creep them,
'Way up to your chin.
Open up your little mouth
But—(pause) do not let them in.
Open them, shut them, open them, shut them,
To your shoulders fly.
Then like little birdies let them flutter to the sky.
Falling, falling, falling, falling,
Almost to the ground.
Quickly pick them up again and turn them round and round,
Faster, faster, faster, faster,
Slower, slower, slower, slower,
Clap!

Eency Weency Spider

Eency weency spider went up the water spout.
   (Thumbs and forefingers make climbing motion)
Down came the rain and washed the spider out.
   (Both hands go up and down)
Out came the sun and dried up all the rain.
   (Raising hands slowly and make a circle with fingers
   touching above head)
So the eency weency spider went up the spout again.
   (Repeat first motion)

I Have Ten Little Fingers

I have ten little fingers
And they all belong to me,
I can make them do things.
Come and watch and see.

I can shut them up tight,
Or open them wide,
I can put them together,
Or make them all hide.

I can make them jump high,
I can make them jump low,
I can fold them quietly,
And hold them—just so.

Here's a Ball for Baby

Here's a ball for baby, big and soft and round
   (Make a circle with thumbs and middle fingers)

Here is baby's hammer, Oh, how he can pound.
  (Hammer with one clenched fist over the other)
Here is baby's music, clapping, clapping so!
Here are baby's soldiers, standing in a row.
  (Hold out hands with fingers outstretched)
Here's the baby's trumpet, toot-too-too-too-too!
  (Hold hands in front of mouth, as a trumpet)
Here's the way that baby plays at peek-a-boo.
  (Cover and uncover eyes with hands)
Here's a big umbrella to keep the baby dry.
  (On vertical forefinger of one hand place horizontal palm
    of other hand, making an umbrella)
Here's the baby's cradle, rock-a-baby-bye!
  (Make cradling motion with arms)

Hands on Hips, Hands on Knees

Hands on hips, hands on knees,
Put them behind you, if you please,
Touch your shoulders, touch your toes,
Touch your knees and then your nose.
Raise your hands way up high
And let your fingers swiftly fly.
Then hold them out in front of you
While you clap them, one and two.

Clap With Me, One Two Three

  (Played with hand motions only)
Clap with me, one, two, three,
Clap, clap, clap, just like me.

Shake with me, one, two, three,
Shake, shake, shake, just like me.

Roll with me, one, two, three,
Roll, roll, roll, just like me.

Snap with me, one, two, three,
Snap, snap, snap, just like me.

Fold with me, one, two, three,
Now let them rest quietly.

Five Fat Turkeys Are We

(If there are four children, say four fat turkeys, etc.)
Five fat turkeys are we.
We have slept all night in a tree. (Palms at side of head)
When the cook came around we couldn't be found. (Shake heads)
That's why we are here, you see. (Nod heads)

Let's fly, fly, fly to the tallest tree. (Make flying motions with arms)
There we'll be safe as safe can be. (Arms crossed on chest)
From the cook and the oven, you see. (Arms crossed on chest)
It surely pays on Thanksgiving days (Shake finger in warning)
To sleep in the tallest tree. (Palms at the side of head again)

Five Little Squirrels

(Older playgroupers can each take a part and learn the right line.
If there are only four children, the mother can take the fifth part)

>Five little squirrels sat in a tree.
>The first one said, "What do I see?"
>The second one said, "A man with a gun!"
>The third one said, "Oh, oh, let's run!"
>The fourth one said, "Let's hide in the shade."
>The fifth one said, "I'm not afraid!"
>Then bang! went the gun, and away they did run.

Some books for playgroup age children

This list includes good children's books sold in all price ranges.

ABC, COLOR, NUMBER AND SHAPE BOOKS

ABC
Knight, Hilary
Golden Press

Bruno Munari's ABC
Munari, Bruno
World

Inch by Inch
Lionni, Leo
Ivan Obolensky

Over in the Meadow
Langstaff, John
Harcourt, Brace and World

Smiley Lion, The
Baker, Marybob
Golden Press

Color Wheel Book, The
Fletcher, Helen J.
McGraw-Hill

I Like Red
Bright, Robert
Doubleday

Little Blue and Little Yellow
Lionni, Leo
Ivan Obolensky

Toy Book, The
Kaufman, Joe
Golden Press

Kiss Is Round, A
Budney, Blossom
Lothrop

Let's Imagine Thinking Up Things
Wolff, Janet and Owett, Bernard
Dutton

Shapes
Schlein, Miriam
Wm. Scott

BOOKS ABOUT ANIMALS

Animals of Farmer Jones, The (ill.)
Rooster Struts, The
Scarry, Richard
Golden Press

Angus and the Cat
Angus and the Duck
Flack, Marjorie
Doubleday

Baby Animals
Williams, Garth
Golden Press

Cat Book, The
Wild Animal Babies
Daly, Kathleen
Golden Press

Everybody Eats
Everybody Has a House
Green, Mary
Wm. Scott

Great Big Animal Book
Great Big Wild Animal Book, The
Rojankovsky, Feodor
Golden Press

I Can Fly
Krauss, Ruth
Golden Press

This Is the Way the Animals Walk
Woodcock, Louise
Wm. Scott

Golden Shape Books

Farm Book, The
Squirrel Book, The
Fox Book, The
Bear Book, The
Tiger Book, The
Cat Book, The
Dog Book, The
Pfloog, Jan

Bunny Book, The
Scarry, Richard

Parrot Book, The
Gergely, T.

Turtle Book, The
Crawford, Mel

Bug Book
Dugan, William

BOOKS ABOUT FAMILIES AND FEELINGS

Big Brother
Zolotow, Charlotte
Harper

Cats Have Kittens, Do Gloves Have Mittens?
Schurr, Cathleen
Knopf

Daddy Days, The
Simon, Norma
Abelard-Schuman

First Night Away From Home
Company's Coming for Dinner
Brown, Myra Berry
Watt

Friend Is Someone Who Likes You, A
Anglund, Joan Walsh
Harcourt, Brace and World

Grandfather and I
Grandmother and I

Buckley, Helen
Lothrop

House for Everyone, A
Miles, Betty
Knopf

I'm An Indian Today
Hitte, Katheryn
Golden Press

Laurie's New Brother
Schlein, Miriam
Abelard-Schuman

Let's Be Enemies
Udry, Janice M.
Harper

Little Bear (series)
Minarik, Else
Harper

Little Red House, The
Skaar, Grace
Wm. Scott

Papa Small
Lenski, Lois
Walck

Play With Me
In the Forest
Ets, Marie
Viking

Switch on the Night
Bradbury, Ray
Pantheon

Which Horse Is William?
Kuskin, Karla
Harper & Row

BOOKS ABOUT TRANSPORTATION AND MACHINES

All Aboard the Train
Big Red Bus, The
Kessler, Ethel and Leonard
Doubleday

Big Book of Fire Engines, The
Big Book of Real Boats and Ships, The
Big Book of Real Building and Wrecking Machines, The
Big Book of Real Trains, The
Big Book of Real Trucks, The

Zaffo, George J.
Grosset & Dunlap

Boat Book, The
Kaufman, Joe
Golden Press

Boats
Lachman, Ruth
Golden Press

Clear the Track
Magic Michael
Slobodkin, Louis
Macmillan

Giant Nursery Book of Things That Go, The
Zaffo, George J.
Grosset & Dunlap

Great Big Car and Truck Book, The (ill.)
Scarry, Richard
Golden Press

Great Big Fire Engine Book, The (ill.)
Gergely, T.
Golden Press

Little Auto
Little Train
Little Airplane
Little Fire Engine
Lenski, Lois
Walck

Little Red Caboose That Ran Away, The
Curren, Polly
Wonder Books

Red Light, Green Light
MacDonald, Golden
Doubleday

Rolling Wheels
Elting, Mary
Wonder Books

Wonder Book of Trains, The
Wonder Book of Trucks, The
Peters, Lisa
Wonder Books

BOOKS ABOUT THE CHANGING WORLD

All Falling Down
Zion, Gene
Harper

Carrot Seed, The
Krauss, Ruth
Harper

City Noisy Book, The
Country Noisy Book, The
Winter Noisy Book, The
Summer Noisy Book, The
other Noisy Books
Brown, Margaret Wise
Harper & Row

Gilberto and the Wind
Ets, Marie Hall
Viking

The Snowy Day
Keats, Ezra Jack
Viking

Sunshine Book, The
Federico, Helen
Golden Press

Where Does Everyone Go?
Fisher, Aileen
Crowell Collier

White Snow, Bright Snow
"Hi, Mr. Robin"
Rain Drop, Splash
Others
Tresselt, Alvin
Lothrop

HUMOROUS BOOKS

Are You My Mother?
Eastman, P. D.
Random House

Away Went Wolfgang!
Kahl, Virginia
Scribner's

Caps for Sale
Slobodkina, Esphyr
Wm. Scott

Cat In the Hat, The
Cat In the Hat Comes Back, The
Seuss, Dr. (Theodore Seuss Geisel)
Random House

Do Baby Bears Sit In Chairs?
Kessler, Ethel and Leonard
Doubleday

Dragon in a Wagon, A
Rainwater, Janette
Golden Press

Harry, the Dirty Dog
Zion, Gene
Harper

How Do You Get From Here to There?
Charles, Nicholas
Macmillan

Millons of Cats
Gag, Wanda
Coward-McCann

Put Me in the Zoo
Lopshire, Robert
Random House

Tobias and His Big Red Satchel
Warner, Sunny B.
Knopf

Too Many Mittens
Slobodkin, Florence and Louis
Vanguard

BOOKS ABOUT WHAT PEOPLE DO

Cowboy Small
Policeman Small
Lenski, Lois
Walck

Daddies, What They Do All Day
Puner, Helen W.
Lothrop

Five Little Firemen
Seven Little Postmen
Brown, Margaret Wise and Hurd, Edith
Golden Press

Little Fireman, The
Brown, Margaret Wise
Wm. Scott

Man in the Manhole and the Fix-It Men, The
Sage, Juniper and Ballentine, Bill
Wm. Scott

My Daddy Is a Policeman
Horwich, Frances
Golden Press

Stan, the Garbage Man
Zion, Gene
Harper

BOOKS ABOUT OTHER COUNTRIES

Jeanne-Marie Counts Her Sheep
Jeanne-Marie in Gay Paris
Jeanne-Marie at the Fair
Françoise
Scribner's

Madeline
Bemelmans, Ludwig
Simon & Schuster

Pelle's New Suit
Beskow, Elsa
Wonder Books

Red Balloon, The
Lamorisse, A.
Doubleday

POETRY COLLECTIONS AND FINGERPLAYS

Animal Mother Goose (ill.)
Scarry, Richard
Golden Press

Book of Nursery and Mother Goose Rhymes (comp. and ill.)
de Angeli, Marguerite
Doubleday

Child's Garden of Verses, A
Stevenson, Robert L.
Grosset & Dunlap

Child's Garden of Verses, A
Stevenson, R. L.
Golden Press

Finger Plays
Holl, Adelaide
Golden Press

I Would Like to Be a Pony (and Other Wishes)
Baruch, Dorothy W.
Harper & Row

My Poetry Book
Pierce, June (comp.)
Wonder Books

Poems to Read to the Very Young
Frank, Josette (Ed.)
Random House

Sung Under the Silver Umbrella
Association for Childhood Education
Macmillan

Tall Book of Mother Goose (ill.)
Rojankovsky, Feodor
Harper & Row

When We Were Very Young
Now We Are Six
Milne, A. A.
Dutton

Wonder Book of Finger Plays and Action Rhymes
Pierce, June
Wonder Books

SHORT STORY COLLECTIONS

Believe and Make Believe
Here and Now
Another Here and Now
Mitchell, Lucy S.
Dutton

Nutshell Library, The
Sendak, Maurice
Harper & Row

Read to Me Storybook
Read to Me Again
Child Study Association
Crowell Collier

Told Under the Blue Umbrella
Association for Childhood Education
Macmillan

CHAPTER 11

Talking and Listening

THE playgroup-age child is involved in a monumental job—learning that intricate and difficult symbol system by which people communicate: language. He is building a vocabulary and learning rules of grammar and usage. He is learning to use language to express his own thoughts and ideas, and he is learning to listen to other people's directions with understanding. In the course of your playgroup morning, there are many ways you can help the children in their struggles to master the complexities of language, some while they are involved in other activities, and others by means of enjoyable activities expressly designed to help children talk and listen well.

Talking

ENCOURAGING CHILDREN TO TALK

Some children will happily talk on and on, even if nobody is listening. Others need help and encouragement in order to gain confidence. You can help these children by taking the time to talk to them during their activities, asking questions and, if need be, helping them form their answers. You can often encourage a child by repeating a phrase that he has used himself; if you are willing to use the same words he used, then the words must have been the right ones, he will feel, and begin to be braver about speaking out. Presenting two alternatives when asking a question will also help a child who is hesitant about committing himself with words. "Was it snowing or was it raining outside?" you might ask, instead of "What's the weather like outside?"

Be observant when the children arrive at your house for playgroup. Is someone wearing a new dress, an unusual shirt, pigtails? Has someone had a haircut? Does someone have a bruised knee? All of these are opportunities for engaging children in conversation. Your interest in these details will be pleasing and flattering and they will be more likely to talk to you freely about their other interests.

If your child has had an interesting experience, encourage him to tell his playgroup about it. It is best to give him a concrete object to take along as a reminder, to show the other children and the mother in charge. For this reason, try to pick up some small souvenir whenever you do something special with your child: a postcard from the museum, a guidebook from a tour, a menu from a restaurant, a seashell from the beach, or even just a receipt from the department store.

ENLARGING VOCABULARIES

Children of playgroup age are greatly interested in words and meanings and the playgroup mother can capitalize on this interest to help the children enlarge their vocabularies. The most obvious, straightforward way to increase the children's vocabulary is simply to inform them of the names of things you see together in the course of the playgroup morning. You may be sure that the children want to know the names of things: this has been their principal occupation from the time they were babies. When painting, name the colors when you bring them out. When working with clay, don't be afraid of words like moist and pliable. (But be sure you show or explain what the words really mean.) When you make jello, introduce words such as dissolve and thicken.

Nursery rhymes present an unusual opportunity to stimulate children's interest in unfamiliar words. Many of the traditional nursery rhymes contain one or two unfamiliar words that most children do not stop to question. You can bring their attention to these words, and then experiment with substituting other words for the unfamiliar word. The humor of this will not be lost on even the youngest playgrouper. For instance, most children learn "Jack and Jill" at an early age, without ever wondering what the word *crown* really means. Some assume that it means the golden thing kings wear on their heads and don't question why Jack was wearing one. Tell them that *crown* is another word for head, and then try out how the poem sounds if you say "Jack fell down and broke his head." The children learn something about the selective nature of poetry, and get into the habit of questioning words they don't understand, instead of just ignoring them. Other examples of unfamiliar words in traditional nursery rhymes:

Goosey, goosey gander, *whither* shall I *wander* . . .
The queen of hearts she made some *tarts* . . .
    Said Simple Simon to the pieman, let me taste your *ware* . . .
She gave them some *broth* without any bread . . .
The queen was in the *parlor* eating bread and honey . . .

USING CORRECT GRAMMAR

It is important for young children to gain confidence in their ability to say what they want and have grownups understand them. If they are interrupted to correct their grammar, they may become discouraged. It will certainly not help their self-confidence. If a child makes a mistake, uses a plural instead of a singular (for instance, "I'm pretending I'm a mice."), it is easy to say the correct form casually in your answer ("Are you a city mouse or a country mouse?") rather than to stop the child and tell him he has made a mistake. If children hear grownups speaking correctly, they eventually learn grammar by imitation. They do not have to be corrected in order to learn.

INTRODUCING FOREIGN WORDS AND PHRASES

There are many reasons why foreign languages should be introduced to children at an early age. The fact that the preschooler is actively engaged in the learning of his own language equips him for learning words in any language. Awareness of foreign words also gives them a clearer idea of the function of words as symbols for objects, actions or feelings. Children have a way of mixing up words and what they stand for. Somehow the word "chair" *is* a chair, not just a word. But if *le chat* and *el gato* and *the cat* all mean the same, then not one of them really *is* the furry animal—they are all equally symbols for it.

Bilingual books and books with foreign words interspersed in the English text are available for preschool children. There are also delightful records of French, Spanish or German folk songs for children, and some which combine English and a foreign language. Your playgroup will enjoy listening to these records and will pick up many foreign words, and even whole songs, if you will help them with the hard words.

DICTATION

A way to increase children's interest in words and confidence in their own speaking abilities is to let them dictate stories, poems, songs, letters or ideas to you. Children delight in the idea that you will write down what they say. It makes them feel important, and reinforces the idea that written words are symbols for spoken words, just as spoken words are symbols for things, and that those mysterious squiggles on the paper have a definite meaning that might be interesting to learn to decipher some day. You can simply tell a child: "You tell me what to write down on my paper and then I'll read it back to you." Then write down everything he says, even nonsense syllables such as ga-ga and boo-boo. (You can, however, unobtrusively correct any grammatical mistakes, just as you do when speaking to a child.) When you read it back to the child, point to each word as you read it and ask the child if that's just what he said. If he wants to make changes, go along with him.

If one of the children in your playgroup is sick, the group will enjoy dictating a group letter to him and the sick child will be happy to receive a letter of his own. You may need to guide them a bit, giving suggestions as to what they might tell their absent friend. This creates a good opportunity for a trip to the post office to buy a stamp and mail the letter.

A group of four-year-olds might even dictate a whole playgroup book, over a period of time, painting illustrations, etc.

SIMILES

A word game that encourages children to think about words and meanings and that can elicit some strikingly original, poetic responses involves suggesting a simile for the children to complete in their own words. For instance, the mother begins, "As quiet as . . ." and gives each child a chance to complete the sentence. "As quiet as flowers, as a snake, as a bit of rain, as when you sleep," are some of the similes children have come up with. As hard as . . . , as deep as . . . , as noisy as . . . , as easy as . . . , the possibilities are enormous. It is best to start this game at an appropriate moment; when a loud noise just startled everybody you can suggest, "That was as loud as . . ." If you are caught in the rain you can try, "This rain is as cold as . . ." You can also try playing with specific things to compare. If you see a rabbit at the zoo, you might try, "His nose looks like . . ." If the children do not respond to this game, they may be too young, and you should wait a few months.

Listening activities

Learning to listen with understanding and to follow directions are important parts of young children's preparation for school, for reading and, indeed, for all their future activities. There are many simple games you can try with your playgroup that will help develop their listening abilities, and be fun as well.

WHAT SOUND IS THIS?

The children close their eyes and the mother in charge makes a familiar sound. The children try to identify the sound. Suggested sounds to identify: clapping hands, stamping feet, ringing a bell, blowing a horn, tapping a glass with a spoon, rustling paper, blowing bubbles with a straw.

WHAT ANIMAL AM I?

The mother makes an animal sound—moo, hee-haw, etc., and the children take turns guessing what animal it is. After the first few times the children can also take turns making the animal noises while the others and the mother guess what animal it is.

LITTLE SIR ECHO

One child at a time is chosen to be Little Sir Echo. The mother says a simple sentence, loudly, and Little Sir Echo must repeat it, a little more quietly if he can.

GIANTS

When the mother calls out "Giants!" the children stretch up high to be as tall as they can be, when she calls "Men!" they stand naturally, arms hanging loosely at their sides, when she says "Dwarfs!" they must crouch down as low as possible. Later the children can take turns being leader. Many other versions of this game are possible, simply by choosing three animals—elephant, kangaroo, bear—and explaining to the children what activity—swaying at the waist, hopping, stalking—to do when the words are called out.

RHYMING GAMES

Tell the children you are going to say some words and they are to tell you which ones rhyme, or sound alike. Then say cat, hat, dog; moon, spoon, knife, etc. Another version children enjoy involves making up couplets with one rhyme omitted, such as:

I'm thinking of a word that sounds like feet.
When suppertime comes it's time to _____.

I'm thinking of a word that sounds like hat.
I say meow, so I'm a _____.

I'm thinking of a word that sounds like red.
When I'm sleepy, I go to _____.

CHAPTER 12

Blocks

BLOCKS are the most versatile of all the materials and toys used by playgroup-age children. Ideally, at least one type of block should be available in every playgroup home.

There are two basic types of building blocks. The most common are the standard wooden *unit blocks,* sometimes called kindergarten blocks, that come in a variety of shapes. Then there are the *large building blocks.* These are made either out of wood or out of cardboard. Large, hollow wooden blocks come as squares, rectangles and ramps, and they can make enclosures large enough for children to get into—but these blocks are usually more suitable for outdoor use. Hollow cardboard blocks are also large enough to build child-size buildings.

The wooden cubes with letters marked on their six sides are often referred to as alphabet blocks, but they are not really building blocks. Their uniform size does not allow for much variety in building, and this in turn limits their value to children a great deal.

Wooden unit blocks

Wooden unit blocks are available in both soft and hard wood. Hardwood blocks are long lasting and hard to splinter. With ordinary use they will outlast your children's childhood. Soft-wood blocks are not as durable, but they cost approximately $15 less for 100. You will need a starter set of about 100 for four or five children.

Some unit blocks come in colors, but blocks that are the color of natural wood allow for freer use of a child's imagination.

ACCESSORIES

A variety of toy people, animals, vehicles and dollhouse furniture is used in block play.

Vehicles means cars, trucks, boats, planes and any other transportation toy. It is good to have some unpainted ones that become whatever the child wants them to be. In buying other kinds, avoid hard plastic that breaks and thin metal that has sharp edges. On wheel toys, check the wheels to see that they can't be removed easily. One company makes a pair of wheels and axles which clip onto any commercial unit block and change it into a vehicle.

Toy people—sets of families or community workers—are made of wood or rubber. One kind of wood person is merely an outline with the details painted on. Another is an abstraction, hand carved to suggest a person. Neither kind is flexible. Bendable people that can sit and "walk" are made of rubber. Occasionally dime stores have large bags of unbendable firemen, astronauts, deep-sea divers, etc., pressed out of plastic.

Animals—domestic or wild—are made in the same three ways: of painted or abstractedly carved wood or of very realistic-looking pliable rubber. They too can be found in plastic. Some of your child's stuffed toys may not be too large to use as accessories.

Dollhouse furniture can be relatively inexpensive when made out of plastic, or very expensive, but much more durable, when made out of wood.

Other additions to your accessory collection are rug and linoleum remnants to cover the floors of block houses, Easter "grass" or excelsior to feed to horses and cows, and string to tape to pillars to make gas pumps.

STORING BLOCKS

Try to make every effort to store blocks on open shelves—even if you have to make them out of milk crates bolted one on top of the other. Blocks are difficult to store by size otherwise, and it then becomes difficult and frustrating for children to build something because it is a chore to find exactly the pieces they want.

Group your blocks by size. Make a tracing of each shape on self-stick plastic, stick it to the back of the appropriate shelf, and the children will know where to put the blocks away. Label the accessories in the same way, whether they are stored on the shelf, in boxes, or in vegetable bins that stack on top of each other.

Leave a sanding block on top of your block shelves, and the children can be taught to sand rough spots on blocks as they put them away. The children enjoy the responsibility of taking care of the blocks, as well as the pure fun of sanding.

Value of blocks

BLOCK BUILDING AS AN ART

Because of the great variety of shapes they come in and because they are cut the same width and thickness, blocks can be fitted together to make a great number of designs. These can be angular or free form. For children who have problems using the messier art materials, blocks can provide their main chance for artistic expression.

If allowed to build as they want, children are often satisfied making a design, as they painted designs at the easel, rather than building actual houses, barns or garages. Block building can be artistically beautiful in the same way that real buildings are beautiful.

BLOCKS AS TOYS OF SKILL

Blocks cannot be used haphazardly. Sloppy stacking usually results in a collapsed building. It takes careful planning and careful building, learned through experience, even to stack blocks into a stable pile, much less into a more complex construction.

It takes skill to find the block a child needs, to tell him how far apart he can put two blocks and still be able to bridge them, and to show him that two unit blocks can be used in place of a double unit if all the double units are already in use.

BLOCK BUILDING AS NOTE TAKING

Older children who learn new facts can jot them down in a notebook. Playgroup-age children can reconstruct in blocks what they have seen and heard. Bridges, skyscrapers, airports and neighborhood stores are all a part of this review and study.

BLOCK BUILDING AS A MEANS OF MAKE-BELIEVE PLAY

Although the bulk of make-believe play occurs in the make-believe corner (see Chapter 15), blocks and their accessories lend themselves to make-believe, too. A house needs a family. The firehouse is incomplete without a fireman. People work in office buildings. Farms and zoos are more than enclosures, etc.

If children don't seem to be working this out for themselves, help them along with leading questions:

"Who lives in this house?"

"Do some of these people (indicate some accessories) work in your building?"

"Does the mommy in your family shop at Sally's store?"

COOPERATION THROUGH BLOCK BUILDING

When children play with blocks, they take them and their accessories from a common supply, which is not limitless. The playroom floor is a common work area to be shared. Even on this simple level, children learn sharing. With the youngest children, who are just learning to play together, you may find it helpful to mark off an area for each child. You can do this either with chalk or with masking tape. "Build inside this square and Jack will build on the other side of the line in his square. That way you will both have room." Soon you will not have to set these limits at all.

As young children get more accustomed to being together, two or more of them often cooperate to construct one building.

A few four-year-olds can build joint communities—houses,

stores, etc.—as well as joint buildings, but this is far more common among children five and older.

It is extremely important to establish early that you will not allow any child to knock down another child's structures, any more than you would let him destroy another child's paintings.

Hints on picking up

One of the main bugaboos of block building is the problem of getting children to pick up and put away their blocks when they are finished. This need not be such a problem. Here are several hints you may find helpful:

• Don't announce cleanup abruptly. If you first warn children that they have five minutes until cleanup, they don't mind so much.

• If you help with the pickup, it usually encourages the children. This kind of job is really a very big one for preschoolers to do alone. While it is important to expect children to clean up after their play, it is more important not to make unrealistic demands on them. If you insist, you may find some children refusing to build because of the cleanup they know comes afterwards.

• Rather than insisting that each child necessarily put away his own blocks, put each child in charge of a shape. George has to put away unit blocks. Susie puts away pillars and columns, etc.

• Young children sometimes enjoy pretending that the shelves are hungry animals that need to be fed.

• Setting up an assembly line and using that word (children love adult-sounding words) speeds the pickup.

• Carts and dump trucks are an aid to pickup.

• Block pickup time is a good time for a song.

Developing basic concepts through block building

DEVELOPING READING READINESS
Matching Shapes

A child needs to acquire many skills before he is ready to read. One of the most important of these is the ability to distinguish one shape from another—for how else can he distinguish a "d" from a "b" from a "p," or an "i" from an "l"? Putting a block on the shelf that contains its silhouette helps to develop this ability.

Using Signs

If a child has built a gas station, it will add to his game if you make a sign that says "Larry's Gas Station" for him to tape to his building. He can use signs saying "Gas" and "Air" for his pumps. If he has built a street in front of the station, he can use a street sign. The more words a child sees and has defined for him (whether or not he recognizes that word a second later), the more he understands that the written word stands for the spoken word.

As you read his sign to him, underline each word with your moving finger, lifting it at the end of each word. Not only are you underlining the fact that words are definite units, but you are showing him that English is read from left to right. These factors, which adults take for granted, must be taught to children.

Whenever you print anything for children—even their names— use both capital and small letters as you would normally, not all capitals. Since reading and writing are related, it is less confusing if your printing looks like the printing in books.

Dictated Stories

When a child asks you to look at his building, or you see a child who has been particularly engrossed during the entire block-building session, or you see a particularly exciting construction, these are good times to take down children's dictations. If you ask one of the children, "Would you like to tell me about your building?" the chances are that he will have a great deal to tell you. As he talks, take down his story, word for word. Watching you take down his story reinforces the idea that written words are symbols. Seeing his own spoken words transformed into written ones makes reading all the more tantalizing.

For children, telling these or any other stories helps them learn to organize their thoughts and speak well.

DEVELOPING MATHEMATICAL CONCEPTS

Numerical Concepts

Understanding numbers means more than being able to count to a high numeral. It means visualizing that the word "two" means //, "five" means /////, "one" means /, and so on. Block building affords many opportunities to better the child's understanding of numbers. "Please pass me three of those blocks," "I'll give you one of these for one of those," "Give me two round blocks," all mean very specific things, and in passing and handling the right number of items he sees one and two and three very concretely.

As you observe block play, you will find many opportunities to help children with these mathematical concepts. There are times when you will quietly correct a child who has used the wrong numeral for the number of objects he was referring to. At other times you will hear a child ask for "some blocks over there." Ask him *how many* he means. "Do you mean *two* (show him two)?" "Do you mean *three* (show him three)?" When you help with cleanup, ask the children to pass you specific numbers of blocks. For playgroup-age children, learning the meaning of one, two, three, four and five is plenty.

Fractions

Using blocks which are made on a unit basis helps children visualize the meanings of words like half, double, etc. Even if they don't know the words, they use the concepts that go with them. They learn quickly through experience that two half-units put together are as long as a unit block. Two units are as long as a double unit. Four half units can be substituted for a double unit, as four units can be substituted for a quadlong. Two triangles also can make a unit block if fitted together correctly, etc.

Non-Numerical Concepts

There are other mathematical concepts besides the numerical ones, such as larger-smaller-medium, low-high, short-tall, first-second-last.

To help children understand these concepts, you might say, "You've built a *tall* building today. Larry's is a gas station, that's why he made his building *lower* than yours."

"Which way is your train going? Then this *first* block is the engine, isn't it? Is this *last* car the caboose or is this a passenger train?"

Successful block building depends on good engineering, which requires understanding a number of basic science concepts. Through the use of blocks, children learn concepts like:

• The broad base of a block makes a steadier base for a construction than does its edge.
• The end of a block makes the least steady base.
• The higher a structure, the more likely it is to fall.
• Carefully stacked blocks generally make a more steady structure than do haphazardly stacked blocks.
• Round things (like columns) roll, while rectangular ones do not.

Children generally find these things out for themselves, but sometimes they need a little help from you. For example, if you see a child repeatedly rebuild a structure that has fallen because he has not recognized some basic engineering concepts, ask him why he thinks his building fell. "Can you lay your bottom blocks a different way?" "Is that helping?" It is important for you to step in before the child gives up in frustration.

Large building blocks

Large blocks are used differently from the smaller unit blocks. Since they are larger, they can be used to make buildings big enough for the children to get into. For this reason, large building blocks are used mostly as an accessory to make-believe play.

If your playroom is small and noise is a problem, you can still find suitable blocks. Hollow cardboard blocks, plastic building boulders and hollow building boards are available in many toy departments. The blocks are usually brick-shaped and come packaged in sets of one size or of several sizes. The boulders and boards are made so that the individual pieces fit into each other rather than stacking. All these are sturdily constructed and some can actually hold the weight of an adult. They are reasonably priced.

If you want a substitute for cardboard blocks that is sturdy enough to build with, but not sturdy enough to stand on, you can wrap cigar boxes or shoe boxes in self-sticking plastic.

Hollow wooden blocks

Wonderful luxury—if you have a large playroom or a back-yard—are the hollow wooden blocks that come in various rec-tangle sizes, and in a ramp shape. The children use them to make buildings, vehicles and furniture, all of which are large enough for the children to get into.

As these blocks are very expensive, you may want to use reinforced beer cartons or milk crates in conjunction with them.

CHAPTER 13

Trips

BY PLAYGROUP age, the young child is beginning to be interested in what is going on in the world beyond his own front door. Once the children have a feeling of belonging to a playgroup and accepting its people and routines, you can begin planning your first organized trip.

Preparing the playgroup

A trip taken without preparation is rarely as successful or meaningful to the children as a well-planned one.

Discuss with the children where you are going, what you are going to see. Sometimes you can even tell them to keep alert for very specific things.

If you have appropriate pictures, display them after you and the children have looked at them and discussed them. If you have an appropriate book, story or poem, read it. If you know an appropriate song, teach it to the children.

Getting there

Taking a trip with your playgroup requires strict safety rules. You must spell these out very precisely so that there is no question about them.

You will probably feel more comfortable if your children walk along the streets in twos. If there are four children in the group, hold the hand of one of the children in the rear pair or perhaps take a position at some point between the two couples. Taking one pair on each side of you takes up too much room on the sidewalk and at the intersection, which can be a hazard. If you are taking five children, you and the fifth child make up the rear of the procession. This does not mean the children cannot break rank when you have found something to investigate. The rule applies to walking, and is most important for crossing streets.

Seatbelts in your car regulate the way children can sit. If you do not have seatbelts, make sure the children are sitting down and back in the rear seat. Kneeling is an invitation to injury if you have to stop short, and it impairs rear vision.

If you are going by public transportation, let the children get on first. As in a car, they cannot be allowed to kneel.

To be sure that the children really understand these instructions, act out taking a trip the right way. Children can pretend to be policemen, or they can be traffic lights, if given a piece of green and a piece of red paper. Line up chairs to be car or bus seats, and practice sitting the right way.

If you feel unsure about managing so many children at one time, ask another adult to accompany you on the trip, rather than giving up the idea altogether.

Trips in the neighborhood

Because his interest up until now has been focused primarily on the things that go on in his home, trips for the preschooler need be nothing more than a walk around the block, an outing in the park, or a walk to the store to buy ingredients for a cooking project. He has so much to learn about his immediate neighborhood that you could plan many exciting trips for the children in the few blocks around your house.

Although the children have walked those same blocks many times before your trip, they usually did so on the way to another destination, and seldom at the leisurely pace which allows real looking and investigation.

If your trip involves seeing part of a store which is not generally open to the public, or if you plan to speak to the storekeeper himself, talk to him beforehand. He can tell you the best time to come, and the children will have a more enjoyable time because they will be welcome.

As eager as young children are, they do have a limited attention span, so don't try to do too much. Make several trips to the supermarket—each with a different focus. Plan to see one or two exhibits at the museum. Don't try to see the entire zoo or farm in one visit, unless it is small.

Stores

If you plan your visit to the stores in a systematic way, the concept of their neighborhood and of very rudimentary geography will become clearer to the children.

A possible plan might be to visit all the stores on one side of the street in consecutive order—one per trip—and then all the stores on the opposite side of the street. How you do it is determined by how your shopping area is laid out.

SUPERMARKET

Watch the goods being delivered.

Watch the boxes being unpacked and stamped.

Look at all the different kinds of machines in the store.

The Produce Department. Why are some things displayed on special cardboard, wrapped in individual papers, or packed with excelsior? Why are some things displayed on crushed ice? Why does the produce man put XX's on the bags of produce after he has weighed them?

The Dairy Department. What kinds of things are sold here? Why are they kept cold?

The Meat Department. Watch the butcher cut and package meat. Why is the meat kept cold? Is it cold in the back, too? How does the butcher keep warm?

BAKERY

Compare the ovens with the ovens at home and the flour sacks with the sacks of flour at home. Notice the quantities of baked goods, the process of baking. What kinds of clothes do the bakers wear? Why?

SHOE REPAIR SHOP

Watch the shoemaker do some repairs. Try to have something that needs fixing. What kinds of machines does he have? What kinds of materials does he use? Try to get some scraps to take back for collage.

DRY CLEANER

What kinds of smells are found there? What kind of machine does he use for ironing? How does the cleaner know which clothes are yours? How can he get the clothes down from the high racks?

PET STORE

What kinds of pets does this store have? Are there any unusual ones? As pet stores do not always have pets on display, be sure that you have made an appointment in advance, or call to find out if the pets are in the window.

FLORIST

What kinds of plants are there? What kinds of smells are there? How does the florist keep cut flowers from dying? Buy a plant and find out how to take care of it.

GARAGE

Watch the gas being pumped into your car's tank. Watch the gas pump itself. What is happening? Why did the bell ring?

Try to see a car being raised with a hydraulic lift, or a tire changed.

Take the children with you when you have the oil and tires of your car checked.

What kind of clothes do mechanics wear?

The community

POLICEMAN AND CROSSING GUARD

Within walking distance of your house there is probably an intersection or a school where there is a policeman (or crossing guard) on duty. Watch what he does. How does he tell the traffic (pedestrians) to go? To stop?

Try to make arrangements with him ahead of time to talk to your children and let them get a good look at his uniform.

MAILMAN

Make arrangements to meet your own mailman at the pick-up box nearest you, and watch him distribute mail.

Go to the pick-up box at delivery time, and the mail box at pick-up time, if these occur during playgroup hours.

Buy a stamp and mail a letter at the post office. Children of playgroup age are not allowed in the back of most post offices, but they can see a good deal if they look through the window of the parcel-post counter.

Watch the packages being weighed and mailed.

BUS DRIVER (CONDUCTOR)

Sit near the driver of the bus (or the subway conductor). Watch what he does. Look at his uniform.

If the end of the run is not too far from your stop, perhaps he could talk to your children during the few minutes he waits there.

FIRE STATION

Some fire departments have open-house days. If yours does not, make an appointment ahead of time.

Do not insist that the children get on the equipment, even if they are invited to. Climbing on an engine can be frightening for some preschoolers.

Look at fire hydrants and fire escapes.

If you live in an apartment house, there may be fire doors, fire extinguishers or sprinklers to show the children.

LIBRARY

Take the children to the children's section of the library. Let them browse.

Show them that all the books have letters, or letters and numbers on them. Why?

Perhaps your library has a storybook hour during playgroup hours?

How does the librarian know which book you have? Take out some books so the children can see the procedure.

SANITATION MAN

It may not be possible to see garbage men, street sweepers or snow-plow drivers in action, as much of their work is done early in the morning.

If you do see them, have the children observe how they are dressed. Why do they wear gloves?

If your community has alternate-side-of-the-street parking, show the children the sign and relate it to street cleaning.

DEMOLITION SITE

Why is this building being knocked down? How?
What will go up here on the vacant lot?

CONSTRUCTION SITE

What kind of building is going up?
What are the girders for?
What kind of machines can you see? What do they do?
How do the men dress? Why?

REPAIR SITES

Observe surface or underground repair sites. What is being fixed? What equipment is in use? How are the men dressed? Why?

What is under the street (or sidewalk)? Where did the rocks and dirt come from? Try to explain to the children that where the city now stands was once country.

A WALK AROUND THE BLOCK

Depending on where you live, you may see some or all of the people and places mentioned above if you take your playgroup for a walk around the block. Even if you don't, you can turn such a walk into a useful and enjoyable trip.

Are the houses (buildings) all the same height? Style? Color? Are they made of the same material?

What different kinds of entrances do they have?

Do they all have fire escapes? If not, why not?

Do you see any workmen on any of the buildings? What are they doing?

What kind of clothes are they wearing? Why?

What kinds of traffic signals can you find? What does Red mean? Green? Yellow? One way? Stop?

How many different kinds of trucks can you see on your walk? What are they delivering? How are the men dressed? How are heavy things taken from the trucks?

Trips outside the neighborhood

MUSEUM

Many communities have both science and art museums. Some have special exhibits for children. Don't try to see everything all at once.

FARMS

For the city child, farm animals are as exotic as wild ones. A farm is very exciting to children, especially if there are some animals they can pet, feed or hold.

ZOOS

There are some compact little zoos especially geared for little children. These can be seen in one visit, but a larger zoo can be overstimulating if you try to see too much. Tell the children they won't be able to see everything, and that there will be other trips to the zoo.

AIRPORTS

Watch airplanes taking off and landing. How do people get on and off a plane? How does a plane get its fuel?

How does a plane change in size and sound the farther away it gets? How does a plane change its size and sound the closer it gets?

HARBOR

What kinds of boats can you see?

Why do some boats have smokestacks? Some sails?

What moves a rowboat? A motor boat?

Why do tugboats have tires all around them?

What does it smell like near the water?

Why are the birds dipping their beaks in the water?

How do people get on and off the boats?

How is cargo put on and taken off a boat?

Try to take a boat ride.

After the trip

Your trip will not be over just because you have returned home. You will be seeing information learned on the trip during block building, dramatic play and art sessions from then on.

But you need not wait for the children to initiate the use of this information. There are many things that you can do to help them fully register what they have seen.

DISCUSSION

Have a free discussion with the children about what they have seen. What is something they saw that they liked? What did they like about it?

If the children bring back some small souvenir, it will help them remember. A register tape, the bag that animal food came in, a picture postcard from a museum are examples of token mementoes.

GROUP STORY

Write a group story about the walk or trip you have taken.

MUSIC

For music time, plan a dramatization of the trip. For example, let each child be something seen on the trip and let the children guess what he is.

Learn some appropriate songs.

DRAMATIC PLAY

Let the children act out the story of their trip. It can be the story they dictated to you earlier.

ART

You may suggest to the children that they draw or paint something about the trip. They may want to do individual pictures or they may really enjoy a group painting or mural at this time.

CHAPTER 14

The Playgroup Outdoors

WHENEVER the weather permits, it is good to spend part of the playgroup morning outdoors, in your own backyard or in a nearby park, field or woods. The children need the greater freedom to move and shout and run around that they have outdoors, and the mother in charge often finds the group easier to manage when they are outside.

Walking in the park or woods

Children's curiosity and eagerness are well-known phenomena and so it comes as a surprise to some grownups that children are not by nature keen observers. In fact, while children are sharp-eyed about the things that directly concern themselves—a change in their rooms, a microscopic scratch on their finger, a worried look on their mother's face—they are quite unobservant about the world around them. If their interest is stimulated in an enjoyable way, however, they begin to see, hear and smell more, and in the process, to begin to move away from the limiting self-centeredness they have known until now.

Of course an outing to the park with a group of preschoolers cannot be run like a college field trip. The children will want to do a lot of running around and climbing and jumping and rolling, and this opportunity for physical activity is one of the main purposes of the outing. But as you are walking through the park or woods to your destination, or as you are resting under a tree, you can bring the children's attention to many different aspects of their environment.

BIRDWATCHING

Getting your playgroup interested in birds will make every outing more exciting for you and the children. In the spring and summer, even city parks have many varieties of birds. Suburban gardens or yards can usually attract many birds with a single birdfeeder and some suet attached to a tree. If there are woods nearby, the birdwatching potential is enormous. You may think that playgroup-age children are too young to differentiate between different varieties of birds, and of course they will not be able to make difficult distinctions. But a three-year-old can easily learn to recognize the most common and striking varieties of birds: bluejays, robins, pigeons, sparrows, and he will get an enormous kick out of identifying a bird that he knows.

A fine way to introduce birds is with the aid of an inexpensive bird book with good colored pictures of the most common birds. If the children show an interest in looking at pictures of birds, they are off to a good start. They can learn some of the birds just from the book, and recognize them when they see them outdoors. Otherwise, a good procedure is to select a single picture of a bird you are likely to encounter and tell the children that today you are all going to look for a bird that looks just like the one in the picture. They will probably take another look at the picture, now that it has become a game. Take the book along, and when you see the robin, or bluejay, stop and wait until one of the group points it out, or point it out yourself. While the children are looking at the bird, you can help them sharpen their powers of observation by asking questions: "What color is the bird's beak?" "How many feet does it have?" "What do the wings do when it flies?" Anything you can tell the children about the nature and habits of the particular bird you are watching will add to their interest—such as that robins' eggs are blue, bluejays sometimes steal eggs from other birds' nests, or that baby cardinals are brownish when they are born and don't turn bright red until they are almost grown up.

TREES AND FLOWERS

A small paperbound book with clear, colored pictures of the most common wild flowers, and a book of common trees will stimulate interest, and the children will enjoy comparing the real thing with the pictures in the book. Daisies, dandelions, buttercups, violets, daffodils, tulips, forsythia—you will be amazed at how quickly and easily young children learn to identify these flowers, and how proud they are of themselves for knowing them. Trees are less obviously differentiated, and it is likely that young children are not at all aware that one tree is different from another: a tree is a tree, they think. It is up to you to point out differences in bark, size, shape and structures of the leaves, the angles of the branches. You might start with the most obviously different groups of trees—evergreens and deciduous trees—and let the children classify the trees they see as one or another of these groups. Then you can show different-shaped leaves, such as sharply pointed, deeply indented pin-oak leaves and smooth, oval-shaped elm leaves. Pressing leaves between sheets of newspapers under a heavy pile of books is fun sometimes, especially for the older playgroupers.

But identifying and classifying are not the only activities you can do with your playgroup, in regard to plants and trees. You can help the children understand some of the basic structures of plant life on your outings. The nature and function of roots is a whole area that will interest your playgroup if you stop and look closely at some roots. The simplest beginning is to uproot a plant or flower, perhaps a dandelion or a clump of clover, showing the children the roots which were under the earth. Explain that the roots are used by the plant to drink water. Ask them where they think plants get the water the roots take in, and don't be surprised to hear answers like "from the water fountain."

Tree roots are more difficult to see, but once in a while a tree uprooted by a storm can be found, with its roots clearly visible. Let the children try to pull a flower out by the roots, to demonstrate another important function of the roots: to keep the flower attached to the earth. After your playgroup has begun to think about roots, you can place a few easily rooted plant cuttings, such as most ivies, philodendra or an ordinary onion, in a glass of water and let the children see how they grow.

In the early spring, the greenness of plants and its relation to sunlight can be illustrated by finding places with uncleared fall leaves and showing that the young plants growing underneath are white while the plants not hidden from the light are green.

In all of your investigations of plants and flowers, you can help your playgroup learn the principles of conservation by discouraging indiscriminate picking of flowers and pulling or swinging from tree branches.

ANIMALS

In city parks and suburban gardens you will probably be limited to squirrels, chipmunks and dogs for your outdoor animal watching. Nevertheless, you can teach the children the principles of quiet observation of wild animals, showing that loud noises or abrupt movements will scare them away. Children enjoy feeding peanuts to squirrels and you can point out how the squirrel eats some of the peanuts and buries others. Ask a question, such as "What parts of the peanut does the squirrel eat?" and the children will watch more carefully.

OTHER THINGS TO LOOK AT

Look about you with curiosity as you walk outdoors and the children will surely follow your example. Look under rocks and logs to see what is there. Notice the different kinds of soils. Notice different rocks and rock formations. You don't have to keep up a steady lecture to the children, and sometimes it is best to seem' to be talking to yourself about what you have found. Many grownups try to get children's interest by talking with great excitement: "Oh, look! Look at *this!*" Unless the discovery is truly amazing, even to you, it is better to use your natural reaction when pointing out things. Children are quick to resent false enthusiasm. They might fall for it a few times, but they will quickly lose interest in anything you show them thereafter.

COLLECTING

Young children like to collect seedpods, berries, twigs, pebbles, leaves—practically anything. This is not the sort of systematic collecting an older child might do; preschoolers often lose interest in their collection before they get home. But the very act of picking up things and putting them into *their own bag* is very satisfying for them and they will look around much more observantly if they each have a collecting bag. You might want to get a permanent collecting bag for each child (small, sturdy plastic-lined cloth bags can be bought for under 50¢) and line it each time with a paper bag which the child can take home filled with his things. Some children enjoy sorting out their collection when you get back. An empty heavy-paper egg carton is a perfect sorting tray and a good item to save for playgroup purposes. The collections can also be used for making nature collages, as discussed in Chapter 7.

A WALKING STICK

Try to find a good stick for each playgroup child on outdoor trips. A stick is to drag, to poke into holes, to drop and pick up, to ride like a horse, to fish in an imaginary sea for whales. Unless your park is very well manicured indeed, you will have little trouble finding four sticks, long twigs or branches on the ground. Be sure to check each stick for sharp ends and thorns.

IMAGINARY EXPEDITIONS

If your walk is limited to pretty much the same route each time, and you feel that the children's interest in the things around them is lagging, you can initiate a make-believe game that the children will probably insist on playing from then on, elaborating on it on their own many times afterwards. "Let's pretend we're really walking in a jungle," you suggest and from there on the possibilities to the game are endless. It is hot in the jungle, so everybody needs a fan made out of a large leaf (skunk cabbage is best), a piece of paper or just the hands. There are animals lurking behind the trees—lions, zebras, elephants. The children can pretend to be animals, or ride them or chase or be chased by them. There are monkeys chattering in the treetops. There are bright birds singing and snakes slithering around. For the youngest children you will probably have to supply the information about what the jungle is like and what may be found there. Four-year-olds may be able to supply some details themselves, especially if they watch adventure programs on television. A trip to the north pole, with ice-breaking activities, penguins, seals and the bitter cold to contend with is another good imaginary expedition, especially on a hot day. Other possibilities are a caravan of camels crossing the desert, or a mountain-climbing expedition (bring along a strong rope to make this even more fun), ending with a ceremonious planting of a flag on the summit. There needn't be a jot of realism about your expeditions. You don't need a hill or a rock pile to climb a mountain. The children will lose themselves in the game while walking on a level path, happily puffing and panting as if they were climbing. They may even swim or row a boat the whole way. All the while you are playing, the children are getting an excellent elementary geography lesson, and what's more, they are making headway in the direction you want them to go. If that direction is homewards, this is not always easy to accomplish.

The weather

The weather is a most interesting phenomenon to children, partly because it is forever changing in new and sometimes bizarre ways (imagine seeing snow or hail for the first time), and mostly because it directly affects their lives—whether they can go out, what they must wear, whether they will feel hot or cold or wet. The nature of your outings will depend upon the weather, and there are many activities you can do with your playgroup that take advantage of different weather conditions. At the same time, these activities can help children understand some basic concepts about weather and some of the scientific principles involved.

A WEATHER CHART

You and your playgroup can keep track of the changes in weather on a weather chart, and on the other days of the week your own child will surely enjoy keeping it accurate. This is a standard item in nursery schools, and very simple for you to make for your playgroup. On a large piece of oaktag, paste colored pictures (or draw them yourself) indicating that the day is sunny, cloudy, rainy or snowy, and also, slightly lower down, windy, cold and hot. A different child is chosen to be Weatherman each week and he places colored triangles of self-sticking paper (or any other easily movable and removable sign) next to the picture of the appropriate weather for the day, one for the top group, one or two for the bottom. You will find the children watching like hawks for any weather changes during the playgroup morning, in order to get a chance to change the weather chart.

THE WIND

A balloon on a string is a surefire hit with a young child on a windy day. A kite is more difficult for a playgroup child to manage, but he will enjoy watching you or anybody else flying one.

To start a child thinking about the nature of wind, here are some questions you might ask:

How can you tell it's windy? (I can feel it.)

What other ways? (Things blowing around, dust swirling, flag waving, clouds moving, etc.)

You can point out that you can tell from which direction the wind is coming by watching smoke coming from chimneys, or flags waving.

Some windy morning, take outside with you an assortment of objects to let the children see that the size and shape of things determine whether they blow away or not. You can show that a piece of foil will blow away while a shiny aluminum pot will not, a single tissue will blow away but a box of tissues will not, a block of wood will stay, but a pile of wood shavings will scatter.

AIR

When you have begun to consider wind with your playgroup, you will probably be surprised to discover that the children have no idea that air is something by itself, apart from wind, and that it exists all around. Give each child a small clear plastic bag and show the children how you can catch air in the bag anywhere you want. They will enjoy air-catching, although they will need help in twisting the bag closed to keep the air inside, and they will begin to understand more about the nature and omnipresence of air. Take one of the air-filled bags and let a child punch a hole in it near a pile of paper scraps or wood shavings, and the children will begin to see the relationship between air and wind.

RAIN

There is no reason to cancel your outing on a rainy day, as long as it is not too cold and the children are appropriately dressed in raincoats, hats and boots or rubbers. The simplest activities are fun for children on a rainy day, and they may think up new ones for themselves, such as catching rain in their open mouths, sailing paper boats or bottle-cap boats in puddles, fishing with sticks and string in puddles, or catching rain in paper cups.

If it is not windy take out an umbrella or two for the children to hold and walk under. Young children love umbrellas.

You can bring up the question of what rain is and where it comes from. You can help the children get an idea about it by a few simple experiments:

Heat up water in a pyrex pot, preferably with cup markings, and show how the level goes down after it has been boiling for a while. Explain that the water didn't really disappear but that tiny bits of it got too small to be seen and that this is called *evaporation.*

Show the children a dry lid and then place it on the top of a pot of boiling water. Now show them the condensed drops of water on the lid and tell them this is called *condensation,* when the tiny, tiny bits become water again. These two things together make the rain.

SNOW

Young children require little encouragement to make the most of snow. They enjoy shaping and molding snow in the same way they do clay. They love to shovel snow in front of the house just like their fathers or maintenance men do, their enthusiasm doubled by the fact that they are not only having fun but doing something truly useful, too. Few children can resist making snowballs, helping to make a snowman, making designs in snow.

You can show your playgroup what snow really is by gathering a quantity of clear snow in a container and taking it indoors to see what happens. Let the children touch and smell and taste the snow and then the water from the melted snow. If you have a magnifying glass, catch a snowflake on a black surface and let the children see the crystalline structure of snow.

If you have your own yard

A yard is a great advantage to any playgroup. Not having to go far afield to take the children outdoors makes life much easier for the mother in charge, and having an easily accessible place to let loose and run around makes life easier for the children. If you have a yard, you and the children can actually spend the whole playgroup morning outdoors, if the weather is nice. Just bring everything out—easel, worktable, art supplies, toys. Many art activities, especially fingerpainting, are more enjoyable outdoors, since the children can be messier than they can indoors. Music and dancing can be freer and more spontaneous outside. Two excellent activities that are difficult or impossible inside the house are easy to set up in a backyard: water play and sand play. Chapter 16 deals with these two activities in greater detail, with suggestions for equipment and things to do with the children.

SUGGESTED PLAY EQUIPMENT FOR YOUR YARD

a sandbox and sand-play equipment
large hollow blocks and planks (commercial variety), or pack-

ing boxes, cardboard cartons, barrels, low sawhorses and planks
water-play equipment: galvanized iron tub, plastic tubs, buck-
ets, watering cans, rubber wading pools
gardening tools
a battery-operated portable phonograph
used auto parts: steering wheel, hubcaps, inner tubes (auto or
truck).

<h3 style="text-align:center">A PLAYGROUP GARDEN</h3>

Your playgroup will like having a corner of your yard for a
garden. You can help the children plant easy-to-grow, hardy
flowers and vegetables such as nasturtiums, zinnias, asters, or
carrots and peas. Don't be upset if the children don't follow the
rules of good gardening. Don't try for neat rows. They are sure
to dig everything over again after you have planted. But something always manages to come up and the children are ecstatic.

Outdoor games

Here are some suggested games and physical activities you
can do with your playgroup, either in your own yard or in the
park, playground or field.

<h3 style="text-align:center">BALL</h3>

The coordination of playgroup-age children is usually not good
enough to throw a ball where they aim it or to catch one thrown
to them.

Passing games and rolling games are better than catch. Here
are a few simple games young children will enjoy. You and your
playgroup can make up others of your own. Be sure you use a
large ball for all games.

• Sitting in a circle, the children roll the ball from one to
another.

• Standing in a line, the children pass the ball from one to the
next with their hands held high above their heads.

• The children take positions at some distance from each other,
at a tree or a bush or fence post. One child runs with the ball to

another and hands him the ball. The child with the ball runs to another child's position, while the first child stays where he is.

• Each child has a light bat or sturdy stick and the children hit the ball as if they were playing golf, one at a time.

• The children crawl on the ground and push the ball around with their heads or noses.

HIDE AND SEEK

A very rudimentary form of *hide and seek* never fails to delight little children. You are always *it*. Tell the children to hide, and wherever they go, pretend you are looking for them and cannot find them. Even if they are practically right in front of you, look in a different direction, or up in the air, look puzzled and say, "Now *where* could Jenny be hiding?" Then, in great surprise, you find her, and you begin to search for the next child. The children begin to get the idea after a few games, and really find better hiding places, although some will continue to cover their faces with their hands and consider that they are hidden.

EXERCISES

Ordinary setting-up exercises, so tedious for grownups, are enjoyed by children when they all do them together. Stretching way up high, touching toes, jumping and clapping, lying on the back and sitting up to touch the toes, pushups are all good. Another form of exercise is related to dramatic play: the children jump like kangaroos, fly like airplanes, turn like windmills and sway their trunks like elephants.

FOLLOW-THE-LEADER

This can be played as a circle game or a marching or walking game. One child is picked to be leader and everybody else must follow him or do what he does. Each child must get a turn to be leader. You may have to give the children ideas of actions to do that are suitable to the game: clapping, tapping the head, going around obstacles, hopping up and down and so on. For preschoolers, the main fun of follow-the-leader is being leader and being first, so don't pay too much attention to whether the other children are really following correctly.

BLOWING SOAP BUBBLES

Since little children are very likely to spill their bottles of bubble liquid, a good plan is to bring a small baby-food jar for each child and a large container of bubble liquid, either the commercial kind or simply a half and half dilution of ordinary liquid detergent and water in a closed jar. Then you can pour out a little of the liquid at a time to each child and refill it when they spill it. Be sure you have a wand, bubble pipe or bubble whistle for each child.

When the children have gotten good at really making bubbles, a simple game they can play is the following: one group of children holds the bubble liquid and makes the bubbles, either by blowing or waving their wands. The others try to catch as many bubbles as they can. The children like to take turns being blowers and chasers.

SINGING GAMES

Traditional singing games are a fine outdoor activity. Looby-loo, Ring Around the Rosey, The Hokey Pokey, and Put Your Finger in the Air are familiar ones that young children love. You can adapt other songs they know into simple singing games just by deciding on one motion for all the children to do during the song. For instance, you all sing Pop! Goes the Weasel, and on the word "Pop," all the children jump up as high as they can. In "Jack and Jill," all the children fall down when Jack falls down.

COMPETITION

A word of warning about competition. Young children have a great deal of natural competitiveness. They are continuously comparing themselves to adults and other children and this becomes a part of their motivation and stimulation for learning. But it is not a good idea to stimulate or encourage competition among children at this age, or create additional competitive elements in their lives. Their skills and abilities are still in a precarious state of development, and encouraging them to compete with each other can end up seriously discouraging some children, while unrealistically encouraging others. For this reason the best games for playgroup children are non-competitive, group games where nobody wins, finishes first or does best. The aim is to have fun doing things together, not for each to try to do better than the next.

Dramatic Play

CHILDREN's dramatic play takes three forms. The first is *make-believe play*. This is imaginative, and the children make up their plots as they go along. These plots are often loosely based on some incident they have observed, or a story they like. But essentially they use their own ideas. The second type is *acting out* stories, songs and incidents. Children enjoy doing this, although they are less likely to indulge in it spontaneously. Occasionally children use *puppets* to play roles they usually play themselves.

Make-believe play

UNDERSTANDING MAKE-BELIEVE PLAY

Often when a child makes believe, he pretends to be someone he wants to understand better. He tries to find out what it is like to be a mommy, a daddy, a big sister, a fireman, a policeman, etc. By putting himself in the other person's shoes, he begins to find out what the other person's job is and how he feels—especially about the child himself.

Sometimes a child acts out his secret wishes. If he doesn't like being small for his age, he can pretend to be big. If his big brother bullies him, he can play big brother.

While he is pretending, he also learns to handle some of the negative feelings that adults don't seem to approve of. Occasionally, he uses make-believe play to help get rid of anxieties brought on by scary stories, books and TV programs.

PROPS FOR MAKE-BELIEVE

The more props children have, the better their play can be. If you provide them with equipment used by the people they are playing, they can play the parts more thoroughly and understand them better. Props need not be new or correct to the last detail. Children's imaginations will provide what is missing. With a few crates from the grocery store and additional accessories your make-believe corner can be whatever the children want it to be. Reorganization and a few changed props can convert one kind of corner to another, from one play session to another.

Whatever kind of corner you have, there are some props that are essential and basic to all make-believe games, and should be available at all the playgroup houses.

1—Women's Clothes:
   Shoes—no higher than a medium heel.

Hats	Short-sleeved Blouses
Scarves	Pocketbooks
Gloves	Costume Jewelry—no pins
Veils	Hair Bands
Stoles	

   Skirts, half-slips and crinolines—especially if they have elasticized waistbands.
   Lengths of fabric and elastic bands with which to convert them to clothes.

2—Men's Clothes: If your husband wears large sizes, you may find it more practical to get these from an older boy. Look for

Short-sleeved Shirts	Clip-on Ties
Sleeveless Sweaters	Vests
Hats and Caps	Scarves
Shoes	Gloves

3—*Two* toy telephones. These encourage conversation, and are appropriate to any situation.

4—A bell: either a desk bell, hand bell, or a door bell (or buzzer) hooked to a dry-cell battery. This lets people in for a visit, calls the store clerk for service, announces a fire to the firemen, etc.

5—A length of hose for putting out a fire, watering the lawn, putting air in tires, or filling an empty gas tank, etc. Pieces of old garden hose or a detachable rubber bath spray can be used.

6—Reinforced cardboard beer boxes. These become shelves, chairs, counters, delivery boxes, cars, trains, boats, planes, space ships and any other vehicle needed.

7—An old sheet, blanket or bedspread for draping over tables or chairs to make a tent, wigwam, house, or cave.

Once you have accumulated the basic props for make-believe, try to get as many additional ones as possible. They add great variety to the children's play. The more props you have, the better. Duplicates of any item are always helpful. A few suggestions are listed here:

Workmen's Shirts	Workman's Helmet
Cowboy Shirts	Sailor's Cap
	Fireman's Hat
Eyeglass Frames—without	Eyeshades
glass or plastic	Hard-visored Caps—for
	policeman, mailman,
Tool Chest	pilot, etc.
Lunch Box	Astronaut's Helmet
Satchel or Shoulder Bag—for	Indian Headdress—the chil-
use as mailbag, briefcase,	dren can make these
doctor's case, etc.	Empty Safety Razor, or
	broken electric one

Old Wheel or Flat Pot Lid—for a steering wheel

Doctor's Kit: Don't buy a doctor's kit with plastic parts which come apart or break easily. Make your own by filling an old shaving kit or pocketbook with:

A real stethoscope, which is indestructible, and which *really works*. Some can be bought for as little as $2.95.
Cotton
Empty Medicine Vials: Do *not* use hard candy as medicine. Too many children's medicines look like hard candy, so using one for the other can be confusing and dangerous.

Bandage Strips

Gauze

Nurse's Hat

Used Hypodermic, which you can get from the doctor the next time your child gets inoculated. He will throw away the needle and give you the syringe.

Storing Props

Dress-up clothes and other small props may be kept in a box, but as with all toys, they are used better if they are kept in a place that allows more organization.

Use shelves, strong orange crates, or milk crates bolted together—one on top of the other. A sheet of peg board hung on the wall is a good place to hang clothes. A shoe bag, hung on the peg board or attached to the shelves, is a good investment, too.

Ideas for make-believe corners

DOLL CORNER

Household furnishings scaled down to size are the basics of a doll corner. Try to avoid the flimsy metal or plastic ones so readily available. They may be perfect replicas of the real thing, but they don't last.

The better-built wooden ones are quite expensive. You can make your own by using milk crates.

Many of the other props needed for the doll corner can be borrowed from your kitchen.

Ideally, your doll corner should have:

• Big, washable dolls with clothes that have big hooks and eyes or snaps for easy dressing.

• A small broom and dustpan.

• Small pots and pans—Many dime stores carry good-quality aluminum pans big enough to cook just one portion. Their cost begins at 25¢, and they are much sturdier than the pieces in the toy cooking sets.

• Dishes—Painted metal dishes rust, and hard plastic ones break. It is better to get either aluminum, stainless steel, or soft plastic dishes. Your best choice may be plastic cups, saucers and bread-and-butter plates made for adults.

• Flatwear—Stainless steel forks, spoons and soup spoons from the dime store, or from an old set, are sturdier and easier to manage than the minuscule sets sold for children.

• Two telephones.

• Play food—This includes empty cans, boxes, cartons and eggboxes that real food came in. Plastic coffee-can tops fit #2½ cans, so they can be refilled. Playdough (see Chapter 7) should be available.

• Kitchen utensils—Rolling pins, cooking spoons, spatulas.

• Iron and ironing board—Buy a sturdy toy iron (not the electric kind). Even a good one is not expensive. Also get a sturdy ironing board. You may find that an adult sleeve board is your best buy, or may even have one.

• Rocking chair.

• Table and chairs—for tea parties.

• Doll's bed. Any box will serve the purpose if it is large enough for your biggest doll.

Your playroom is probably your child's bedroom, so there is a big bed that can be used when the children play doctor, or when mommies put real children to bed. If your playroom is elsewhere in the house, you will find it useful to make a doll bed big enough to lie on.

To make a child-size doll bed, start with an old carriage mattress. Cut a piece of plywood ½″ longer and ½″ wider than your mattress. Screw on 2″ legs that can be bought commercially, or use four blocks of wood 2″ x 2″ x 2″. One advantage of the carriage mattress is the availability of bedding for it.

• Kitchen furniture: stove, sink, cupboards. Any piece of furniture can be made from a basic building unit. The basic unit consists of a sturdy orange crate, or of two milk crates bolted together, one on top of the other.

• Stove: Mark four burners on the top box with an indelible felt-tipped marker. For a super model stove, bolt two units together, side by side.

• Cupboards: Basic units.

• Sink: Bolt together two basic units, side by side. Remove the top slats from *one* top crate (you may have to saw them off).

DIAGRAM 15-1

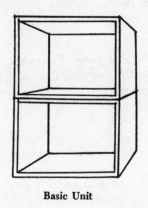

Basic Unit   **Stove**

Insert a rectangular dish pan into this remodeled top crate. The top of the other top crate can be covered with linoleum or self-adhesive plastic to make a drain board.

STORE

A few easily saved items can be the basis for a wonderful store.
- Empty cans, boxes and containers.
- Cardboard box for delivering groceries.
- Paper bags.
- Pad and pencil for scribbling pretend orders.
- Two telephones, one for calling in the order, one for taking it.
- Cardboard and plastic produce baskets such as berries, apples, tomatoes and grapes come in—in many sizes.
- Real food. Lend the children some hardier produce, like carrots, apples, potatoes and onions that don't come in savable boxes.
- Play money and a money box. Buttons and green construction paper can be money in a pinch. A cash register, provided that it is not flimsy, is a nice addition.
- Counter and shelves. A table can become the checkout counter, and reinforced beer cartons can become stock shelves. If you want something more permanent, bolt together some of the basic

units mentioned under doll corner. If need be, cardboard cartons, a wide window sill, a shelf, a tray can all become shelves.

FIREHOUSE

Playing fireman is a favorite make-believe game. Fireman's hats may be the only item you have to buy. You probably already have or can easily get the other accessories.

- Fireman's hats, one for each child.
- Two telephones.
- Piece of hose.
- Fire truck built from hollow blocks, chairs, or reinforced beer cartons.
- Hand bell to tell the firemen that it is time to go to a fire; and it can also serve as the siren warning people to get out of the way.
- Steering wheel. An old training wheel from a bicycle or a flat pot lid makes a good steering wheel for the driver of the truck.
- Ladder (opt.). If your child has some kind of climbing apparatus or a sturdy stepstool, this can be used to convert a firetruck into a hook and ladder truck.

DIAGRAM 15-2

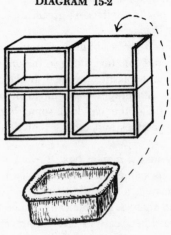

Sink

How you can help in make-believe play

Even though children do most of their make-believe playing on their own, there is still a lot you can do to help them along. Usually you don't have to participate actively—although on occasion the children may actually assign you a part. In general, your role will be subtler.

If you have listened and observed as unobtrusively as possible, your common sense will tell you when it is time to step in and how to do so.

ASSIGNING ROLES

At times children have trouble getting started, especially if they are younger and not used to playing with other children. In such cases you can assign the roles. Hand Bobby a box and suggest that he be a delivery boy. Remind Susie and Anne that mommies go marketing, and tell Dick that the game needs a grocery man. Beginning players often need directions as specific as these to get the game going. The successful game gives the children more confidence, and you may not have to give such specific directions again.

HELPING ONE CHILD JOIN THE GROUP

At other times, it may be only one child who is having trouble getting started. He may not know how to get into the game. "Why don't you ring the doorbell? Pamela is fixing a party and parties need company. Here are some candles for her cake." The child will feel more secure because he has something to contribute, and the contribution helps to make him more welcome.

SUPPLYING MORE INFORMATION

Sometimes the game starts well, but later falls apart. The children gradually lose interest and drift away, or the game becomes wild and uncontrollable. This sometimes happens because the children don't have enough facts to keep them going.

For example, in a game of fireman, the children may get bored with running back and forth putting out fires. When you see the game beginning to deteriorate, it is time to step in. "Firemen don't spend all their time fighting fires. They spend a lot of time at the firehouse. What do you think they do there?" The children may know, but if they don't, tell them. "They clean the firehouse. They wash and polish the trucks." Provide the children with rags or sponges to wipe down the trucks, and a small dish of liquid wax to polish them. This little bit of added information is enough to get the game going again.

After an incident like this it is time to visit (or revisit) the firehouse and to read a book like *Fireman Small.* In general, take children on trips (see Chapter 14) and read them stories related to home and community subjects. By doing these things, you will give the children more facts to incorporate into their play.

PROBLEMS THAT MAY COME UP

Much of make-believe play brings many of children's deeper feelings closer to the surface. This is one of the great values of make-believe. But children often have to be helped to cope with these feelings, especially if they take a form that is harmful, dangerous, or destructive—to themselves or to others. At the same time, they must not be made to feel guilty about *feeling* the way that they do. What can *you* do?

Reflect His Feelings

When a child is angry or unhappy, it is often enough to reflect his feelings to him, like a mirror. "You are angry, aren't you?" Or better yet (provided that you know the reason), "You are angry because you didn't get the first turn at driving the fire truck. That's why you're throwing things around." Words have a magical meaning to little children. Calling a feeling "angry" relieves a lot of the anger.

Reassure Him

Being reminded that all people, even grownups, sometimes get angry, is reassuring to an angry child, and helps him feel better.

Stop Destructive Behavior

When one child has attacked another, or has destroyed something the other child has made, no playgroup mother should stand at the sidelines. "I know you are angry, but you may still not hit Anne. You know I wouldn't let her do it to you, and I can't let you do it to her." If you can find a face-saving way for Susie to get back into the game, all the better.

Usually, "Why did you hit Anne?" is not a useful question. Susie may really not know, even if she thinks she does. Many times it has nothing to do with Anne at all.

Stop Verbal Aggression

When aggression takes the form of name-calling, or "I won't be your friend," or "Don't be his friend," children must be reminded that they can hurt each other "inside" as well as "outside"; and that you can't allow this any more than hitting.

Help the Aggressive Child

As you feel yourself getting mad, it is extremely important to remember that the child who is the aggressor is often more frightened than the child who has been hit. He doesn't have the comfort of moral indignation, and it is a frightening experience to be out of control. After you have made sure that the other child has not really been hurt, you might sit down with the aggressive child. Hold him (if he will allow it). Talk to him, and encourage him to talk to you. Talking it out is always helpful. If he is not a very verbal or talkative child, it may help him to let out his energy by cutting paper, pounding clay, playing a drum, painting on the easel, or hammering pegs.

DEVELOPING CONCEPTS THROUGH MAKE-BELIEVE PLAY

Even make-believe play which has little adult direction can help children develop certain important concepts.

Identities and Sex Roles

Dressing in adult clothes helps children clarify identities. Am I a boy or a girl? Will I be a lady or a man? A mommy or a daddy?

Encourage boys to wear men's clothing and girls to wear
women's clothing, especially when the play is home and family
oriented. If a boy insists on wearing women's clothes (or vice
versa), don't make an issue of it. Perfectly normal preschoolers
sometimes like to play in clothing of the opposite sex. The inci-
dence of this is much less if you have plenty of dress-up clothes
of both kinds.

Costumes such as the clothing of firemen, astronauts, cowboys
fall into a different category. Their appeal is created by their
colorfulness and the excitement of the roles associated with them.
It doesn't hurt to suggest that Judy be a cowgirl or the ranch
cook; or that maybe Anne might someday be the first lady astro-
naut; or that it *is* fun to pretend to be a fireman, since there aren't
fireladies.

Correcting Misinformation

Children of three and four are full of misinformation and con-
fused facts. You can overhear a great deal of this when you are
observing make-believe play. "I'm going to *cook* this cake," announces a three-year-old, placing her playdough on a burner of
the doll corner stove. "Doesn't your mommy *bake* cake *inside*
the *oven?*" you might ask casually.

"Where is your daddy?" asks one four-year-old mommy of
another—clearly meaning "husband." Mixing up family relationships and the names for family members is only one confusion
common among playgroup-age children. Once you overhear that
kind of remark, you can make a mental note to talk to the children
about daddies and mommies, husbands and wives, grandmas
and grandpas. This concept is a little too complicated to handle
with an offhand remark on the spot.

Sometimes when children are deeply involved in a game of
make-believe, even a casual correction might interrupt the flow
of the game. If that is the case, wait until a later time to correct
the confusion.

Acting out stories

Acting out is another way children use dramatics. It differs
from make-believe play in that the idea which is the point of
departure is not completely original with the children.

BEGIN WITH FAVORITES

The best things to begin with are the children's favorite nursery rhymes, poems, stories or songs. The ones you select should have a simple plot that includes movement.

After you have reread a familiar rhyme (or whatever you have chosen) tell the children they will have a chance to do what the poem says. Help them choose roles, and if there are more children than roles, the extra children can join you in saying the rhyme. On the next rhyme, they can get roles.

Repeat the verse, slowly and clearly, as the players mime their roles.

A poem like "Jump or Jiggle" from *Poems to Read to the Very Young* is also great fun to act out. The first time you read it to the children they can enjoy the sounds. The second time they can become the animals that "jump," "hump," "jiggle," "wiggle," "stalk," etc.

Stories like *The Three Bears, Are You My Mother?* or *Caps for Sale* are naturals for acting out because they are simple and involve action.

ACTING OUT TRIPS

Going on a trip can be less awesome if the trip is acted out beforehand. You and the children can act out waiting for lights, going on buses, looking at animals or looking at the fire engines, or whatever the trip involves.

IMAGINARY TRIPS AND EVENTS

The idea behind a dramatization can be entirely imaginary. You can, for example, announce to the children that today "We are going on a pretend trip to the beach. Let's pack." Ask the children to add to the story. As each child adds his contribution, the group acts it out.

The group can "Take a Walk," "Get Ready to Have a Party," "Have Lunch at a Restaurant," etc.

AVOIDING TV THEMES

Children's TV is full of super heroes. Imitating these characters is often a matter of complete mimicry. There is little leeway for creative dramatics. For the few hours a day the playgroup is together, it is a better idea to encourage the kinds of dramatics that allow more creativity on the children's parts.

This is equally true of dramatics involving gunplay. Many nursery schools do not allow guns in the classroom—not because of any pacifist point of view, but because a gun (especially the ultra-realistic ones on the market today) by its very presence structures the plot so rigidly that the children don't really have a chance to use their imaginations freely.

And while it is true that a finger can be a gun substitute, many children do not bother to make the substitution and can easily be distracted into more constructive play. Through a book like Lois Lenski's *Cowboy Small,* playgroup cowboys can find out that gunplay is a nonexistent part of the modern cowboy's life, but that he leads an interesting life anyway.

Puppets

Children enjoy puppets either for variety, or to use if a role is too frightening for them and they want a little distance from it.

The simplest hand and finger puppets are the best for playgroup children. Marionettes are too complicated. An entire set of finger puppets can be bought for under $3. Hand puppets cost $1 and up, depending on the material and detail. Chapter 7 has a number of suggestions for puppets the children can make.

Here are some puppets and puppet stages which are too difficult for children to make, but very simple for you.

HOME-MADE PUPPETS

Darning-Egg Puppet

Glue felt features on a darning egg. Use yarn or wood shavings for hair. Push the handle downward through a man's handkerchief (or a piece of fabric that size) which serves as clothes for the puppet. The puppet is held and manipulated under the handkerchief.

Rubber-Ball Puppet

Paint features on a small, hollow rubber ball. To manipulate it, the child pushes his index finger up through a hole cut in a man's handkerchief or fabric, and through a hole in the rubber ball.

DIAGRAM 15-3

Person Hand Puppet

Activities
DIAGRAM 15-4

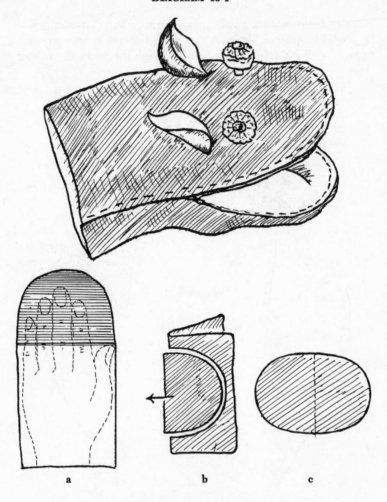

a

b

c

Animal Hand Puppet

Apple, Potato or Carrot Puppet

Cut felt features and push them into the plant with a straight pin. With an apple corer make a hole in the bottom of the plant big enough for a child's index finger. Manipulate this puppet just like the hollow ball puppet.

Hand Puppet with Face

Trace around your flat hand: second, third and fourth finger together, and thumb and pinkie out. Cut two pieces of fabric this shape and seam them together, leaving the bottom open. If you use felt, it does not need hemming, it is strong and the seams won't ravel. Use buttons for eyes, yarn for hair, and embroider a mouth—or glue on a felt one.

Animal Hand Puppet

Trace an outline of your hand according to diagram *a*, cut two pieces this shape, and seam them together as far as the shaded part of the pattern. Fold a piece of contrasting felt, trace the shaded part of the pattern onto it, and cut around the tracing, following diagram *b*. Stitch along the fold of the oval piece that results (diagram *c*). Insert this oval piece into the open arch of the main puppet piece and stitch it in place. Use yarn, buttons or more felt to add details.

PUPPET STAGES YOU CAN MAKE

• A table lying on its side is the easiest puppet stage. The puppeteer hides behind the table, using the top table edge as the stage.

• A sheet taped to the front of a table, hanging all the way to the floor, is another easy stage. The table top is used as the stage floor.

• A doorway chinning rod or a rod for instruments (Chapter 7) can be used as a curtain rod. Adjust it to a level just above the height of your tallest child. Using large hooks (such as shower curtain hooks) hang an old sheet or drape for the puppeteer to hide behind. The puppets are raised above the curtain.

• A grocery box with the top and bottom flaps removed becomes a puppet stage. Lay it on its side on a table so you can look though it. The puppets are manipulated from the back.

• A grocery box with both top flaps and *one* bottom flap removed can be made into a TV set. Tape the remaining flap shut. Attach buttons or bottle caps to the front with paper fasteners

to make the dials. You can attach a cloth to the back for a
backdrop.

DIAGRAM 15-5

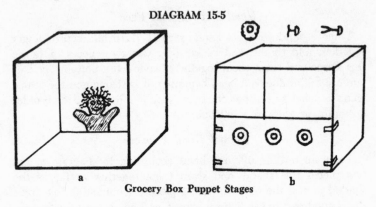

a   b

Grocery Box Puppet Stages

HOW TO BEGIN

*If the children in your playgroup have never seen a puppet
show,* you will need to put one on so they can have an idea how
puppets are used. A couple of puppets talking to the children
and getting them to join in on songs the entire group knows, is
puppet show enough. Children who have seen puppet shows
will enjoy it too.

The younger playgroupers are happy being puppeteers for
dolls, stuffed animals, or the simplest hand puppets. Direct questions or conversations to these puppets, and the children will
answer for them.

For older playgroupers, you can plan an acting out activity
based on a story, rhyme or poem. When you tell the children
that it will be acted out, tell them that the puppets will be the
actors. Let them help you decide which puppets will play which
role, and which puppeteer will manipulate each puppet.

You can *combine art and puppets* by helping the children decide which roles in a story they would like to play, and then
helping them make their own puppets, following one of the
suggestions in Chapter 7.

If you *leave puppets on the shelves* so that they are accessible
to the children, they will take them and use them to produce
impromptu puppet shows.

CHAPTER 16

Water and Sand

MOTHERS who have watched their young children in the bathtub or the sandpile don't have to be convinced of the fun they have playing with water or sand. Even babies who have an initial dislike or fear of water generally overcome it by playgroup age, and splash around with the same enjoyment as children who enjoyed water from the beginning.

Water

Water is soothing. It can calm the angry child, and relax the tense one.

Water is easy to work with. It gives. It changes shape. Unlike wood and paper, and even clay, it offers no resistance. It does what the child wants it to.

There is no "right" way to play with water. There may be a few rules about not spilling water intentionally or splashing wildly in the house, but there are no comparisons a child can make with any other child's way of playing with water. In playing with water, he can feel successful. And once he feels successful in one area, he is much more willing to try his hand at other things.

At a time in his life when his mother is asking him to stay dry, a difficult request, it is relaxing to a child to be invited to get his hands and arms (and occasionally, in a wading pool or sprinkler, all of him) wet.

WATER PLAY IN THE HOUSE

Setting Up

If your bathroom is large enough for the children to avoid the
danger of banging their heads against the basin every time they
stand up, large pans or a galvanized tub put on the floor are
perfect for water play. (Bathtubs are too deep.) Lay a thick
carpet of newspapers, and you won't have to worry about children slipping. A laundry room is equally good. Otherwise, you can
use any room (preferably one that has a linoleum floor) if you
put plenty of paper and a plastic throw under the basin of water.
The basin need not be directly on the floor. It can be on a table.

The children's clothes should be covered with plastic aprons,
and their shoes can be covered with boots or even plastic bags,
or if you wish, they can be removed completely.

Suggested Accessories

- A bar of floating soap or some soap flakes
- A set of measuring cups
- Funnels
- Meat baster
- Rotary egg beater
- Piece of hose
- Empty squeeze bottles from medicated soap or baby lotions
- Boats
- A variety of objects that float and others that do not float:
corks, sponges, wooden ball, hollow ball, rubber eraser, etc.
- Food coloring
- Bubble pipes, one for each child
- Small watering can with a spray attachment

Ways to Play With Water

Children play with water as a part of other types of play. The
sink in the doll corner is for doing dishes, washing clothes, or
washing babies, but while the playgroupers are doing these
houshold tasks, they are also indulging in water play.

Many recipes, such as playdough, that call for quantities of
water as one of the ingredients, also allow children to play with
water while doing something else.

Little children do not look upon washing their hands as the routine function adults consider it to be. For them, it is another opportunity to indulge in water play. So be sure to allow ample time for washing up.

Nursery-school teachers have long noticed that many children who try to avoid most kinds of cleanup, are perfectly willing to scrub tables and floors, even after fingerpainting or clay. Washing boards, brushes and paste pots are other clean-up jobs that also qualify as water play techniques.

Because water is so popular, cleaning up after water play is not as formidable as it might seem. The children who enjoyed playing with it in the first place enjoy playing with it further in the process of mopping up.

WATER PLAY OUTDOORS

If you have no yard of your own, you are limited by what your neighborhood park offers. Once the weather has turned warm, some parks offer sprinklers for children to run in. Still others have wading pools. Some parks have neither, so your playgroup may have to be satisfied with carrying pails of water from the drinking fountain to the sandpile. You can, of course, take bubble pipes with you to the park.

If you have a backyard, you can provide the children with the same tubs and accessories they used indoors for similar play. They also enjoy wading in an inexpensive plastic wading pool or playing in a spray which has been attached to your garden hose. Watering your lawn or garden with spray cans, or especially with your hose, is another enjoyable form of water play for children. This will mean even more to them if they have their own garden to tend.

Sand

Sand, like water, is easy to work with. It acts like a fluid and pours, changing shape as it is poured. It has give, and offers little resistance.

Sand can be played with in many ways. There is one basic

safety rule about not throwing sand, but aside from this there is no right or wrong way to play. For this reason sand offers security to young children who are not yet sure about what they can do, and how well they can do it.

Sand can be dampened to make a different kind of material, somewhat similar to clay. Wet sand can be used to build towers, castles, holes and tunnels, or it can be formed into mud pies. Like fingerpaints, it invites children to be messy at a time when they may be worrying about keeping clean.

SAND PLAY IN THE HOUSE

There is no reason to limit sand play to the outdoor sandbox. You can set up sand play on a modified scale right in the playroom.

Fill a pan with high sides, such as a dish pan or a roasting pan, and provide the children with accessories such as measuring cups, funnels, spoons, strainers, small cars, empty shakers, sugar and coffee scoops and the like. Use a small sprinkling can to moisten the sand.

SALT—A SUBSTITUTE

If for some reason you find it difficult to get hold of sand, salt makes a very satisfactory substitute. By far the best kind of salt to use is the large-grained salt usually called Kosher salt. A tray of salt and the same accessories that are suggested for sand make a good game for playgroup-age children, who can stick with it for a surprising length of time.

The two drawbacks of playing with salt are that it dissolves when it gets wet, and will sting in a cut or scratch when damp.

SAND PLAY OUTDOORS

Any park playground will have a sandbox. In some parks there are certain sections where children are allowed to dig the soil.

In your own yard, you can allow the children to play in a certain section of the yard or you can provide a sandbox—or both.

BUILDING A SIMPLE SANDBOX

Mark off your sandbox on the ground. Dig a channel along the layout markings and fit a lath into each side of the layout. Nail the laths together at the corners to give you the frame of the sandbox. Line the bottom and sides with heavy-gauge vinyl (to prevent the sand from mixing with the soil, and to keep the sand dry). Fill the box with beach sand or construction sand. When it is not in use, cover the sandbox with another piece of vinyl that you have weighted at the corners. Otherwise rain may get the sand wetter than you want, and neighborhood dogs may dirty it.

ACCESSORIES

- Pails and shovels
- Coffee cans and other containers
- Small gardening tools
- Strainers and sifters
- Spoons and scoops
- Gelatine molds and pie tins
- Watering cans
- Cars and trucks
- Spatulas

Developing concepts through water and sand

While children play with water or sand, you can point out to them some of the following principles:

WATER

- Generally, heavy things sink and light ones float.
- Hollow things float until they fill with water.
- Water won't go up a baster unless you squeeze the bulb, and when you do that, air bubbles come out of the end of it.
- Blowing air into a pipe full of soapy water makes bubbles.

• Certain things like sponges, cloth and paper sop up water.

• Water takes the shape of its container.

• Water itself has no color. It takes the color of its container or whatever is dissolved in it.

• Using sets of measuring cups helps children see relationships between volumes: Two pink cups (½ cups) will fill one white cup.

SAND

• Things that are bigger than the holes in a sieve won't go through.

• Things like salt and sand that are made of small pieces will pour like water and take the shape of the container they are in.

• If you wet sand, the pieces stick together and you can mold it or build with it.

• If you look at sand through a magnifying glass, some of the pieces are shiny.

Index